EXCELLENCE IN THE WORKPLACE

By Robb Thompson

Unless otherwise indicated, all Scripture quotations are taken from the *New King James Version*, copyright © 1982 by Thomas Nelson, Inc. All rights reserved.

Scripture quotations marked *KJV* are taken from the *King James Version* of the Bible.

Scripture quotations marked *NAS* are taken from *The New American Standard Bible*. Copyright © 1960, 1962, 1963, 1968, 1971, 1972, 1973, 1975, 1977 by the Lockman Foundation. All rights reserved.

Scripture quotations marked *AMP* are taken from *The Amplified Bible*. *Old Testament* copyright © 1965, 1987 by Zondervan Corporation, Grand Rapids, Michigan. *New Testament* copyright © 1958, 1987 by The Lockman Foundation, La Habra, California. All rights reserved.

Scripture quotations marked *NIV* are taken from *The Holy Bible: New International Version*®. NIV®. Copyright © 1973, 1978, 1984 by International Bible Society. Used by permission of Zondervan Publishing House. All rights reserved.

Excellence in the Workplace
ISBN 1-889723-24-X
Copyright © 2002 by Robb Thompson
Family Harvest Church
18500 92nd Ave.
Tinley Park, Illinois 60477

Editorial Consultant: Cynthia Hansen
Text Design: Lisa Simpson
Cover Design: Greg Lane

Second Printing, 2003

TABLE OF CONTENTS

FOREWORD

When Robb Thompson speaks, leaders listen.

Recently, I sat at a table surrounded by a select group of leaders well known for their integrity, excellence, influence, and unparalleled productivity.

One by one, each leader shared his encounters and experiences with Pastor Robb Thompson. The conclusion was always the same. No one could recall meeting any human with a higher standard of excellence. I understood their profound respect. Robb is the most consistent, giving, and trustworthy friend a person could ever have.

His integrity is impeccable.

His standard of excellence has yet to be surpassed by anyone I have known in my thirty-six years of world travel.

His generosity is legendary...as yet unequaled by any other known leader.

He is the greatest seed sower I have ever known.

He is one of the very few who has mastered both the Law of the Seed and the Law of Excellence, the two greatest laws on earth.

He is the most qualified leader I know to mentor us on the Law of Excellence.

He has forever changed my life.

Now...this unforgettable book will forever change your life.

Dr. Mike Murdock

INTRODUCTION

I should tell you right from the beginning — my passion is excellence. I press for it every day. I push for it. I pursue it. I desire it. I ask God to show me ways to become better in everything I do. I don't want to be the same tomorrow as I am today.

But I'm not just interested in becoming a person of excellence myself. My desire is to get rid of every trace of mediocrity in your life as well. I want to help you reach a higher level in your walk with God than you have ever imagined. I want you to become everything God intends for you to be!

You see, it's important to have someone in your life who can take you to another level. Very seldom will you get there by yourself. You need someone who is further along than you are, someone to put his hand on your shoulder and help you get where you want to go in life.

That's why I'm interested in helping you focus on becoming prosperous in this life — spirit, soul, and body. That goal is attainable, friend. It doesn't matter who your daddy or your momma was. All that matters is who your Daddy is now! When you understand who your Heavenly Father is, you'll realize that nothing and no one can stop you from becoming a person of excellence in every area of life.

But understand this: Rising to another level in life doesn't just happen automatically or by chance.

Life is built by *choices*, not by a series of chance occurrences. Different choices take you down different paths. Wrong choices take you to places you don't want to go. On the other hand, you can choose on purpose to become everything the Lord wants you to become!

Yes, that choice involves a great deal of change, and it isn't always easy. But once you become willing to do whatever it takes to become the person God has already said you are, *nothing* can hold you back — not worldly pressures, or other people's unbelief, or any demon spirit assigned to trap you in the mire of mediocrity.

Now, don't think for a minute that the message of this book is just a nice little Bible sermon I put together. Everything I'm going to share with you has already produced great dividends for me. If you could have seen me before I knew Jesus and then witness the life I'm living today, you'd understand exactly what I'm talking about!

You see, I got saved as a young man in a mental institution in 1975 after living through a very difficult childhood. I understand what it's like to be abused. Both my parents were alcoholics, as was I by the time I was thirteen years old. By the time I was sixteen, I was also a drug addict. (That was my way of trying *not* to be like my parents!)

So you can't tell me that your background or your childhood experiences are keeping you from becoming a person of excellence. I know you can do it, because I have done it! Today I know who my Daddy is.

I know where I'm going. I am determined to do whatever I have to do to reach the next level of excellence in every area of life. I absolutely refuse to allow myself to be a mediocre Christian.

You have to make that same choice for yourself. You see, what you believe about yourself will determine the outcome of your life. That means you are personally responsible for your future. You have to decide what you want.

Do you want to stay the way you are? Then you'll stay the way you are. It takes action to change, to make things different in your life. If you don't do something to accelerate who you are, you'll never go anywhere. If you just sit around and wait for God to do something for you, nothing will ever be any different. You'll end up waiting till the cows come home, and they haven't even left yet!

Having said all that, I specifically want to talk to you about living as a person of excellence in the workplace. My desire is to help you launch into the pursuit of achieving your full potential as a Christian businessperson or employee. I guarantee you, opportunity is knocking at your door as never before. Becoming a winner in the workplace is easier than ever because there is actually very little competition.

From every direction imaginable, the world is teaching this modern generation to stay mediocre in life. People are being told that they are victims; that they are the way they are because of someone else; that they should be paid a wage just because they show up at work. The quality of their work doesn't matter. Their personal integrity doesn't matter. All that matters is "You owe me my wage, and I'm going to get it from you!"

But God has planned something better for you, friend. He didn't call you to be mediocre, and He didn't call you to lose at anything. According to Second Corinthians 2:14, He has chosen a life for you in which you don't have to be defeated for even one moment: **"Now thanks be to God who ALWAYS leads us in triumph in Christ...."**

I want to help you understand how to not only cause doors of opportunity and promotion to open in your life, but also how to *keep* them open. You don't have to live one second not knowing how you're going to pay your next bill. Your life in the workplace can be one that goes from glory to glory, from faith to faith, and from victory to victory.

However, *you first have to become willing to change.* When you're finally willing to wrestle your flesh to the spiritual floor of your life and make yourself follow the principles of excellence contained in this book, these scriptural principles will change not only your experience in the workplace — they will transform your entire life. Soon people will be saying of you what they once said of Jesus as He walked this earth: **"...He has done everything excellently (commendably and nobly)!.."** (Mark 7:37 *AMP*).

In His Service,
Robb Thompson

★ ★ ★ ★ ★

RISING TO ANOTHER LEVEL

God designed life to be a continual ascension. This is the very reason that today's excellence is tomorrow's mediocrity. Excellence is like the manna God sent to the children of Israel to eat in the wilderness. The manna was fresh, delicious, and nourishing when they gathered it in the morning. But if the Israelites tried to save it for the next day, it became moldy, maggot-ridden, and stale.

So no matter what level you are at today, tomorrow you should be bored with that level and ready to move up higher. You have been created for movement and for change!

Now let's put this in the context of the workplace.

Today's excellence is tomorrow's mediocrity.

This means you shouldn't let a day go by without looking for ways to become a better employee, employer, entrepreneur, clerk, or executive. You can decide every single day to push away from mediocrity as you press toward the next level of excellence in your life's journey.

Most Christians don't understand what it takes to achieve that next level. They think success in the workplace is a great mystery they can't attain. But the truth is, most people don't achieve the next level for one simple reason: *They aren't willing to make the sacrifices and changes that are necessary to propel them forward toward promotion and success.*

How about you? How serious are you about going to another level in the workplace, or even in life for that matter? Have you invested in that goal by deciding to do whatever it takes to become what God wants you to be at your job? What have you done to prepare yourself in order to get where you want to go in your career?

You see, if you're going to vacate the present level at which you work, you have to choose the hard way and do something different until the new eclipses the old. That's the way it works in the Kingdom of God. The old doesn't just suddenly disappear, never to show up again. Your new life in Christ — God's way of doing things — begins to eclipse your old ways of thinking and acting. Finally, you become more in love with Jesus than with those old, carnal attitudes and habits that have kept you in low-level living for so long. It is that overriding love for the Lord that propels you upward to the next level.

As for me, I always choose the hard way as I pursue the call God has placed on my life. I don't ever choose the easy way because I realize the easy way is deceptive and takes much longer in the long run.

Pursue God Above All Else

So how do you start rising to the next level within the realm of your chosen occupation? How do you get from where you are now to where God wants you to be? (*Note:* As we talk about rising to a higher level in the workplace, remember that these same foundational principles of excellence apply to every area of your life.)

First, you have to remember something:

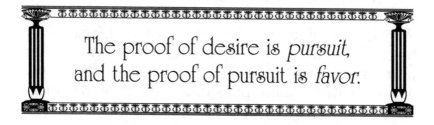

The proof of desire is *pursuit,* and the proof of pursuit is *favor.*

You see, you are only going to possess what you are willing to pursue. You won't obtain your goal of excellence at your job by just talking about it. If you don't pursue it, you won't possess it.

13

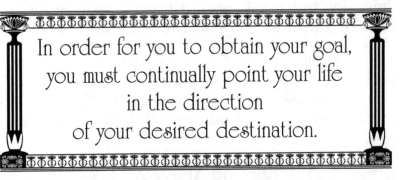

In order for you to obtain your goal, you must continually point your life in the direction of your desired destination.

For instance, we will never cause someone to draw closer to us if we're continually criticizing that person. We will also never receive promotions at our place of employment if we are always talking to the other employees about how terrible it is to work there. You see, our lives will never go in the opposite direction of the way we speak. Therefore, in both these cases, our words and actions are pointing our lives in the opposite direction of our desired goal.

On the road to a higher level in the workplace, our first pursuit must always be the *pursuit of God.* Why is this? Because if we're not careful, after we've been a Christian for a while, it's easy to start pursuing the things of the world through the *avenue* of God rather than pursuing God *Himself.* Jesus said it like this:

"But seek first the kingdom of God and His righteousness, and all these things shall be added to you."

Matthew 6:33

The truth is, *broken focus* is the main thing that keeps us from experiencing the changes we so greatly desire in our lives — and the most dangerous time

14

for this to happen is when everything is going well in our lives.

Consider the way the story of David and Bathsheba all began. David was a king who would go out to war in the spring, just as all the other kings in the region did. But this one particular spring, David stayed home. Why? *Because he lost focus.* He quit pursuing the very thing God told him to pursue. Laying down his sword and his shield, David started wondering what to do with all the time he had on his hands. He eventually found his answer — in the arms of another man's wife (2 Sam. 11:1-4).

We all face the same dangers and temptations. The most treacherous time we'll ever face in our lives is when things are going well. That's when we start thinking, *I need a break. I need to take a little more time off for fun than I've been doing.* We begin to take more vacations. We think we deserve a little more luxury in our lives. It doesn't matter if people consider some of those luxuries wrong; we still deserve them. Little by little, our broken focus starts us sliding down a slippery slope into the abyss of mediocrity that has swallowed so many believers before us.

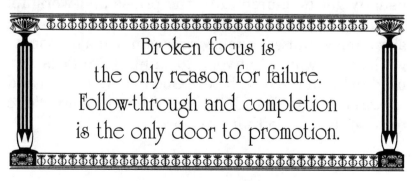

Broken focus is
the only reason for failure.
Follow-through and completion
is the only door to promotion.

15

This problem of broken focus is all too common in the Church. When people first come to Jesus, they pursue Him with all their hearts. I mean, they go after it! They just love to read the Bible. They love to pray. But then, little by little, they start pursuing the things of this world. Soon they're going through each day feeling depressed and guilty. Why? Because they have stopped pursuing God. By breaking their focus, they have broken the universal law that says *motion brings emotion.*

That law works every time. For instance, did you ever see someone get all excited at church about praising and worshiping God? They might even jump up and down and shout, "Oh, thank You, Jesus. Glory to God! Praise the Lord! Hallelujah!" Why is that? Because motion brings emotion.

So if you want to get yourself out of discouragement or depression regarding your job or other areas of your life, just start singing praises to God. Jump, shout, run — do whatever you need to do to break out of that mess and praise the Lord!

Someone might say, "Well, I'll tell you, Robb, we usually get to church after the praise and worship. We used to worship God when we weren't making any money. But ever since we began to make money, we haven't wanted anyone to think we're fools. We used to lie on the floor before God to pursue Him and to worship Him. But things are different now. We're too dignified to do that anymore."

But that kind of excuse doesn't have any merit in God's eyes. He has commanded us to love and pursue Him.

Too often people's eyes get off their goal of pursuing God. Maybe they were excited about God for a while, but then things changed. Everyone started pulling on them at work and at home, wanting them to take on another responsibility. Their phone began to ring night and day. Their eyes wouldn't be open for ten seconds before the telephone started ringing and someone presented them with the first problem of the day.

So it went day after day. At the end of each day, they'd say, "Lord, I promise that tomorrow I'll pursue You. I'll seek You tomorrow, Lord." Then the next day they'd say, "Oh, Lord, I'm sorry — I have too much to do today. I'll have to spend time with You tomorrow."

If that sounds at all familiar, the solution to your problem is simple. Just set your focus back on pursuing God, and relight the fire in your relationship with Him. You see, you can't expect God to do something in your life regarding your career or your job until you do your part by seeking Him first above all else.

I remember when I got saved in that mental institution. For years I had been wrecking my life more and more each day, until finally I began to lose my mind. But then came that day in the institution when I bowed my knee and cried out to God for help.

In less than eight hours, He delivered me from every bondage and transformed my life.

Now, at the time the Gospel was preached to me, I could have said no to the Lord. Or I could have said yes and then never allowed the new creation to manifest in my life. God was waiting for me to make the right choice. As soon as I determined to make Jesus my Lord and Master and to pursue Him at all costs, God moved on my behalf. By the power of His Word, the new began to eclipse the old in my life.

Love the Lord
With All Your Mind and Strength

Deuteronomy 10:12 *(KJV)* gives us God's requirements for us as believers. Certainly these requirements apply to how we act in the workplace:

> **And now, Israel, what doth the Lord thy God require of thee, but to fear the Lord thy God, to walk in all his ways, and to love him, and to serve the Lord thy God with all thy heart and with all thy soul.**

In Matthew 22:37, Jesus adds one more thing to this first and greatest commandment: **"...You shall love the Lord your God with all your heart, with all your soul, and with all your mind."** Then just in case we say we love God but then treat others in such a way that makes our love for God hard to recognize, Jesus gave us the second greatest commandment: **"...You shall love your neighbor as yourself."**

Here's our main dilemma: We may not have any trouble loving God with all our hearts. We may not even have trouble loving the Lord with all our souls. But we find ourselves in trouble when Jesus tells us to love the Lord our God with all that is going on inside our *minds.*

The only way you can obey that command is to embrace the new creation that God has made you in Christ. Old things are passed away, and all things have become new (2 Cor. 5:17). You may ask, "But what about the wrong thoughts that sometimes go through my mind? I'm supposed to love God with all my mind!"

Proverbs 12:5 says something very important about this: **"The thoughts of the righteous are right...."** As a new creation in Christ, I have been made the righteousness of God in Christ (2 Cor. 5:21). So whenever a wrong thought comes across my mind, I immediately remind myself that it was not my thought. Why? Because the thoughts of the righteous are only right.

Are you righteous? Then your thoughts are only right thoughts.

"Well, then, where did this bad thought come from?"

You shouldn't care about where it came from — only about where it's going, and that's out of your mind!

Jesus also said we are to love the Lord our God with all our strength. That word "strength" carries the meaning of *passion*. Remember, motion brings emotion. We are to love God with our motion, or our actions of passionate pursuit.

You have to come to the place where you would never say, "Lord, I love You, but I can't spend time with You today because I have too much work to do." Never again will you say, "Lord, I love You, but..." There are no "buts" when you are pursuing God with all your strength.

When most people first get saved, there aren't any "buts" between them and the Lord. They might even tell their friends, "I'm not going to that social event because I need some time to worship God. You may not see me for a while because I'm going to be on my face worshiping Jesus."

But as time passes, those same people might start saying, "Oh, Lord, I might not have any time for You today. Oh, well — at least I listened to a teaching tape while I was driving to work." Or maybe they say, "Well, I'm just too tired." Meanwhile, they keep watching movies that keep them up too late!

Some Christians protest when they hear me talk like this. They ask, "Well, gosh, do I need to go to church all the time?" When those believers first got saved, they would have never asked Jesus a question like that. They were like David when he said, "It felt right when they said to me, 'Let us go unto the house of the Lord'" (Ps. 122:1).

You see, we have to decide whose house we're going to — God's house or Beelzebub's house? We can't kid ourselves that the choice doesn't have to be made. We are somewhere all the time, so we have to choose: "Am I going to God's house? Or am I going to the house of poverty, the house of sickness, or the house of sin? I'm always going to be at someone's house, so whose house will it be?"

Delight Yourself in God

In your pursuit of God, you also need to understand this: You must *delight* in God. This brings us to a very important excellence principle:

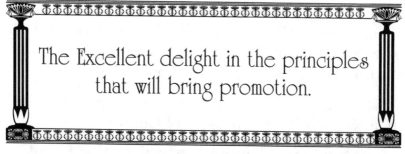

The Excellent delight in the principles that will bring promotion.

You see, I always want to know what it's going to take for me to receive a promotion from God. In every situation I face, what gate do I need to pass through that will bring promotion into my life? Ten years from now, I don't want to ask those whom God has put over me, "What do you think I've been doing wrong these past ten years that kept me from being promoted?" I want them to tell me right now what I need to do so I can do it right the first time.

I don't want to go through life like a ball in a pinball machine, bouncing from one side to another, trying to figure out what I should be doing to get to the next level in life. All God has to do is tell me what I need to do to be promoted, and I'll "X" out everything else in my life that runs contrary to what He has said.

David certainly lived this way before God. He wasn't perfect by any means, but he always put his passion in the direction of his desire. In Psalm 26:8, David said this:

Lord, I have loved the habitation of Your house, and the place where Your glory dwells.

David was saying, "I have loved where Your honor resides, God. I revere You. I honor You. I'll not take You for granted. I'll not rebel against You, Lord. I love the habitation of Your house."

Then in Psalm 27:4, David once more talked about his passionate pursuit of God:

One thing I have desired of the Lord, that will I seek: that I may dwell in the house of the Lord all the days of my life, to behold the beauty of the Lord, and to inquire in His temple.

Notice David *didn't* say, "I have a list of things I've desired from God." He said, "*One thing* I have desired of the Lord, and that one thing is what I will seek after."

That's what I mean when I say that David put his passion in the direction of his desire. He determined,

"The one thing I have desired of the Lord — to dwell in His Presence and to know Him intimately — is the one thing I will seek. That is my passion and my pursuit."

You see, most Christians you'll ever meet in your life don't have a clue about how to move in the direction of their desire. In fact, they don't move at all in their walk with God. There's nothing going on with them. The last touch of God they experienced was the day they got saved — *if* they even experienced one then!

But David said, "Oh, Lord, I love to go to church to praise and worship You. I wouldn't think of showing up forty minutes after praise and worship starts, because it is my passionate desire to behold Your beauty and Your glory."

Your Father God wants you to worship Him. Why? Not because He is egotistical, but because He wants you to know the joy and fulfillment of being in His Presence.

David also says this in Psalm 84:1,2:

How lovely is Your tabernacle, O Lord of hosts!
My soul longs, yes, even faints for the courts of the Lord; my heart and my flesh cry out for the living God.

Can you imagine loving God so much that you get depressed to the point of fainting when you can't spend time worshiping in His Presence? Once again we see that universal law in operation: *Motion brings emotion.*

David would have understood why the writer of Hebrews gave us this warning in Hebrews 10:25,26:

Not forsaking the assembling of ourselves together, as is the manner of some, but exhorting one another, and so much the more as you see the Day approaching.
For if we sin willfully after we have received the knowledge of the truth, there no longer remains a sacrifice for sins.

You see, throughout the ages, God's people have always had this problem. That's why Christians who sometimes don't feel like going to church shouldn't think that they're the only ones who have ever felt that way. The only people who have wanted to go to church through the years are the ones who have made a crucial discovery and who therefore say, "Lord, if only I had known earlier that when I press in to You, I become everything You ever wanted me to become and everything I ever wanted to be!"

I'm not saying this just to convince you to attend church. God created church for *you*; He didn't create church for Him. God didn't create you so He could *get* something *from* you. He created you so He could *give* something *to* you.

David goes on to say in Psalm 84:3, **"Even the sparrow has found a home, and the swallow a**

nest for herself, where she may lay her young — even Your altars, O Lord of hosts, my King and my God." David was saying, "Before Your altar — in the fullness of Your Presence — is where I bear fruit, Lord, for I cannot bear fruit in my own strength."

It is your time spent in the Scriptures and in the Presence of God that changes you and ultimately takes you to the next level in the workplace and in every other area of life. Think of the time Moses spent on the mountain with God. God burned His commandments into two tablets of stone, and as Moses focused on those written commandments, his face was lit with the glory of God.

Similarly, when you delight yourself in the Lord and focus on the Word of God, His glory will light up your life. You'll quit thinking, *Lord, when are You going to come through for me at my job?* because you'll realize He's already come through and has just been waiting on *you*!

Someone might ask, "But how can I know the voice of God?" Well, why do you know the voice of your mother or your father? Because you know them. In the same way, the more you press into God, the more you'll recognize His voice.

Jesus said, "My sheep hear My voice and follow Me" (John 10:3). So if a person is having a hard time hearing God's voice, that means one of two things. Either he's hearing it all the time but is confused about what he's hearing — or he isn't one of Jesus' sheep, and he'd better get *that* problem straightened out first!

Love God's Word

There is a second requirement you must fulfill in order to go to another level in your career or business. It's this: *You must learn to love God's Word on a higher level.*

You have to pursue the Word of God with the same passion the psalmist did who wrote Psalm 119. Just look at the way this psalmist spoke of his heart for God's Word:

I will delight myself in Your statutes; I will not forget Your word.

Psalm 119:16

The law of Your mouth is better to me than thousands of coins of gold and silver.

Psalm 119:72

I hate and abhor lying, but I love Your law.

Psalm 119:163

Great peace have those who love Your law, and nothing causes them to stumble.

Psalm 119:165

That brings us to another key to excelling in the workplace and in the other arenas of our lives:

Lord is excellent, and it converts the soul to God's standard of excellence. So if your soul — your mind, emotions, and will — is not being converted to the way God thinks and perceives things, you can know you're not spending enough time in the Word. You haven't injected into your mind and heart enough of the one ingredient that can accomplish the converting.

Next, David says, **"...the testimony of the Lord is sure, making wise the simple"** (v. 7). When he declares, "The testimony of the Lord is sure," he is saying, "What God says will happen. It will surely be!"

You see, God is not in control of your decisions; He has given you a free will to choose which way you will go. However, He is in control of the *consequences* of your decisions, and His testimony is sure. When He says, "This will happen if you do that," it will surely come to pass. That's why you need to learn from other people's mistakes!

Too many people decide they want to learn their own lessons in life, so they end up learning the hard way. I decided long ago that I didn't want to do that anymore. I got tired of getting beaten up by the devil. I'll just wait outside while someone else decides to learn the hard way, and then I'll learn from his mistakes!

We must first believe that what God has said in His Word is true. Then as we read the testimonies of people in the Bible who did something God told them not to do and then reaped the consequences, it

29

will help make us wise so we don't make the same mistakes.

That's in part what David meant when he said the testimony of the Lord is sure, making wise the simple. The Word helps us get to the point in our lives where we no longer have to learn by experience. For instance, a girl is warned, "Sweetie, don't go out with that boy. He's trouble!" But she goes out with him anyway and comes back pregnant, crying, "But he told me that he loved me!" She could have learned the easy way by listening to wisdom, but now she has to live with the consequences of her choice to learn from hard experience.

You see, you have to realize this: *Wisdom is always before the fact.* You may never know of all the right decisions you make in life. But you will always know when you make a wrong decision because you will have to face the negative consequences.

That doesn't mean you should dwell on all those wrong decisions you made in the past. Forget those mistakes. That was yesterday. Remember, your future is ahead of you, not behind you. Let the Word make you wise so you can avoid ever making those same mistakes again!

Next, David said in verse 8, **"The statutes of the Lord are right, rejoicing the heart...."** If your heart is not rejoicing, friend, you haven't learned enough of God's statutes.

Most Christians who are sad or discouraged don't realize how simple the solution to their problem is.

They say, "I just don't feel the joy of the Lord in my life the way I should." So other well-meaning Christians say to them, "Well, come on, we'll just pray together and fix that."

Can you see how silly this gets? The Christian life is not as mysterious as most people think it is. It's simple. If Christians will spend time studying and meditating on God's statutes, they'll get happy!

Someone might say, "But I need pills to get happy."

Well, I'm talking about the best "happy pills" of all — the statutes of the Lord! The Bible says those divine statutes are *right*. That means we are not to argue with them.

Something I learned about Jesus is that He has never lost a case, so I'm not going to question Him. I realize that the excellent approach God with unquestioned obedience. Many times I don't even spend time talking to Him about certain situations I face because I already know the answer. He wrote it down for me in His Word, and whatever He says is right.

Be Willing To Make Sacrifices For the Lord

The third thing you must do in order to rise to a higher level in the workplace and in life is be willing to make sacrifices.

Sacrifice is one of those things many Christians want nothing to do with. When they hear a message on sacrifice, they usually think it's talking about someone else.

But life has to become serious to us, friend. Our walk with God must be real. We can't just go from meeting to meeting saying, "I just love to hear the Word!" without never making the necessary sacrifices to become all God wants us to be.

Why keep hearing the Word if we never act on it? God didn't give us His Word or His Presence to make us feel good. He gave us His Word to entrust us to change future generations. We need to remember that the next time we're tempted to compromise our walk with God in front of our children. The moment we do that, we set something in motion in their lives that can never be regained, for anything passed on to the next generation multiplies.

That's why we must learn how to make sacrifices in order to go to another level in our jobs and in every area of life. This brings us to the next excellence key:

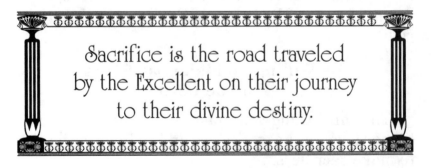

Sacrifice is the road traveled by the Excellent on their journey to their divine destiny.

When men and women of God come to minister at my church, I often ask them to talk to the congregation about the experiences they went through in order to get where they are today. The two most common things these ministers talk about are the sacrifices they had to make in the early years and their determination never to quit serving God, no matter what.

Jesus talked about this kind of sacrificial commitment in Luke 14:33:

"So likewise, whoever of you does not forsake all that he has cannot be My disciple."

What was Jesus saying here? Unless we are willing to walk away from all we have in this life, we do not qualify for His Presence. We will not obtain an audience with God until we are willing to walk away from all the world offers for His sake.

Too many times we have the wrong attitude about our walk with God. We may say, "I want to move on in my journey to the higher life You have for me, Lord." The problem is, we often add, "But, Lord, I want to take this particular thing with me."

That's what Jesus was talking about when He said it is easier for a camel to go through the eye of a needle than it is for a rich man to enter into the Kingdom of God (Matt. 19:24). We can't take the things of this world with us, so we may as well be willing to sow it into God's Kingdom.

In Philippians 3:8 (*KJV*), Paul talked about his commitment to sacrifice all worldly gain in order to gain Jesus:

Yea doubtless, and I count all things but loss for the excellency of the knowledge of Christ Jesus my Lord: for whom I have suffered the loss of all things, and do count them but dung, that I may win Christ.

Paul was saying, "That's how much the things of this world stink compared to knowing God. I count it all dung that I may win Christ." He went on to say in verse 9 (*KJV*):

And be found in him, not having mine own righteousness, which is of the law, but that which is through the faith of Christ, the righteousness which is of God by faith.

You could paraphrase the first part of this verse this way: "That I may be found in Him, not having a righteousness based upon my performance."

Then in verse 10, the *Amplified* version puts it this way: **"[For my determined purpose is] that I may know Him...."** I have a determined purpose. I am focused on getting to know Jesus better. I'm focused. I'm going to another level in fulfilling His call on my life, so don't try to talk me out of it!

Every one of us has to make this decision. We have to establish in our hearts that we want to go to a higher level in God. Otherwise, we may find that the sacrifice it requires is more than we're willing to invest.

Yet even though it does require sacrifice to pursue the next level, we must do it regardless of the cost. If we don't, we have only stale, moldy manna to look forward to!

Be Willing *and* Obedient

Another crucial requirement for going to the next level in the workplace is *obedience*. Isaiah 1:19 (*KJV*) says, **"If ye be willing and obedient, ye shall eat the good of the land."** If we don't want to eat the worst of the land, we just have to stop being disobedient!

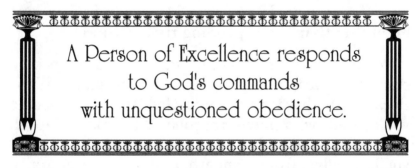

A Person of Excellence responds to God's commands with unquestioned obedience.

Someone might say, "Well, it's hard to always be obedient to my employer, but I still want to eat the best of the land." But he can't have it both ways.

A person of excellence understands that. Therefore, he loves and pursues God with all his heart and soul.

I've learned to respond with unquestioned obedience in my relationship with God. My only question to Him is "What else can I do to be obedient to You?" I'm not looking for ways *not* to be obedient. I'm praying, "Lord, help me to be more obedient."

35

I operate by that same principle of obedience with those over me in the Lord. I don't sit and wait to hear the same thing twice. I don't question them about the wisdom of their instructions. As far as I'm concerned, once it's spoken, it's done.

In John 14:15, Jesus simply says, **"If you love Me, keep My commandments."** His message to us is clear: "If you love Me, you'll do something about it. Your actions will show Me that you love Me. You'll guard My sayings in your life. I won't be an inconvenience for you. If you love Me, I'll be your assignment, your focus, your obsession. I'll be pursued by you. If you love Me, you'd rather quit breathing than stop spending time with Me."

When Jesus starts talking like that, people suddenly start falling off all over the place. Why? Because the higher you go in God, the fewer people you'll find who have reached that higher level. Therefore, the higher you go, the more criticism you'll receive from beneath and the more praise you'll receive from above.

Let's look at some other verses along this line. In John 14:23, Jesus said, **"...If anyone loves Me, he will keep My word; and My Father will love him, and We will come to him and make Our home with him."** Actually, Jesus was saying, "If you love Me, I'll move in with you"!

Then in John 15:14, Jesus said this: **"You are My friends if you do whatever I command you."** Jesus is saying to us, "Do you want to be My friend? If you do, you will do what I say."

We may say, "Okay, Lord, I do want to be Your friend. But can we change that verse to say, 'You're My friend if you *want* to do whatever I command you'?" But that doesn't work. We must be willing *and* obedient to eat the good of the land.

First John 5:3 (*KJV*) confirms this by telling us exactly what it means to love God:

For this is the love of God, that we keep his commandments: and his commandments are not grievous.

That word "grievous" can be replaced with the word "hard" or "difficult." People say, "It's just so hard to obey the Word." No, it isn't hard to do the Word. God's commandments are not hard to obey. But I'll tell you what is hard — the way of the transgressor (Prov. 13:15)!

Finally, in Second John 1:6, it says, **"This is love, that we walk according to His commandments. This is the commandment, that as you have heard from the beginning, you should walk in it."**

I have determined to walk after God's commandments. I'll go after them. I'll pursue them with my all my heart, soul, mind, and strength.

You see, obedience is not an option to people of excellence; it is a way of life. It is the fragrance that emanates from them in the workplace and in every other setting of life because the motto they live by is this: "The answer is yes, Lord. Now what is the question?"

Understand the Power of the Seed

A lifestyle of giving is also required in order for you to go to another level of success in your work and in your life in general. This leads us to a very important principle:

A Person of Excellence understands and embraces the power of the seed.

You must understand and embrace the power of the seed so it can transport you from where you are to where you need to go.

One problem people often have in this arena of giving is understanding *how much* seed they are to sow. These people might find an answer to their dilemma if they would study David's example as a giver.

I personally believe that David was the greatest giver in all the Scriptures. Remember, David was the one who went to the Lord and said, "Lord, I want to build You a house."

The Lord answered, "No, you won't build Me a house because you're a man of blood. I don't want that around My house. However, your son will be a man of peace, and he will build My house."

It's true that David was a man of war and that Israel was at peace during Solomon's entire reign as king. However, you have to understand something: There are times when a nation must go to war in order to obtain peace. This was true in David's case.

Still, when David asked to build God a house, God told him no. But David was such a giver that he found a way around God's "no." David said, "Lord, You may have told me that I couldn't build Your house, but You never told me that I couldn't pay for it!"

Although in this case God wasn't trying to keep David from giving, you can still apply David's response to any person who is a giver. A giver will always find a way around the technicalities people set up to keep him from giving. One way or another, he'll find a way to give. God likes that quality because it reflects His own giving nature. In fact, God created giving for the giver, not for the receiver, so the giver could discover what it feels like to be like God for just one moment.

The closest you'll ever come to feeling like God is the moment you're giving from your heart. That's why it's more blessed to give than it is to receive. The devil knows the power of the seed, so he tries to sow lies in your mind to make you think it really isn't necessary to live a lifestyle of giving.

But if giving was something that really didn't matter, why does the devil keep talking to you about it? I'll tell you why, friend — *because your life is completely dependent on the purity of the seed that you sow.*

Often the reason people can't seem to break through in the giving of their finances is that they have never reached the level of *sacrificial* giving. Instead, they live their lives in the realm of *convenience* giving: "This is what we can comfortably give, and we're not going to give one penny above that amount!"

But if that's their attitude, these people will never reach a new level in life. No one I've ever known or heard of has broken through easily in the realm of giving. The only way a person does break through is by making an uncompromising, unwavering commitment to believe in God's very great and exceedingly precious promises.

Once you break through in your giving, it becomes easy; however, until you do break through, it's the hardest thing you've ever done. But just keep two things in mind as you give: Number one, you are never to question the mission of the seed as set forth by the Scriptures. Number two, you must realize that you will reap in due season if you faint not.

At times you may sow and sow and sow and sow, expecting a harvest that never seems to come. Finally, you get to the place where you don't even care anymore if there *is* a harvest; you're just giving because you love God and want to obey Him.

It is at this point that some of your greatest financial breakthroughs can take place. You see, the moment your focus is back on God instead of your harvest is the moment His principles of sowing and reaping begin to work for you. So never let *anything* take your focus off Jesus. Always keep your focus pure and fixed on the Lord, for only in His presence is fullness of joy (Ps. 16:11).

Surrender to God's Precious Promises

Everything we've talked about so far in this chapter are things you have to diligently pursue if you want to rise to another level of success and prosperity in your career and in your life. Now I want to take you to Second Peter 1, where the apostle Peter gives you specific steps to take so you can prepare yourself for that higher level. To begin with, he says this:

According as his divine power hath given unto us all things that pertain unto life and godliness, through the knowledge of him that hath called us to glory and virtue:

Whereby are given unto us exceeding great and precious promises: that by these ye might be partakers of the divine nature, having escaped the corruption that is in the world through lust.

2 Peter 1:3,4 *KJV*

Notice Peter says that God has called us to glory and virtue. The word "virtue" means *moral excellence*. God has actually called us to live in excellence! How do we fulfill that call? Verse 3 tells us: *through our knowledge of Him who has granted us all things that pertain to life and godliness*. The more knowledge we have concerning Jesus, the easier it is for us to walk in excellence.

Then in verse 4, Peter says in essence, "To enable you to live in moral excellence, God has given you very great and exceedingly precious promises, so that by these promises you might be a partaker of His divine nature." In other words, you need the promises of God if you are going to partake.

Therein lies the problem with many Christians. They have allowed the god of this world to blind their spiritual eyes and keep them from partaking of God's promises. Second Corinthians 4:3,4 (*KJV*) tells us that this is Satan's primary strategy:

But if our gospel be hid, it is hid to them that are lost.
In whom the god of this world hath blinded the minds of them which believe not, lest the light of the glorious gospel of Christ, who is the image of God, should shine unto them.

Paul is saying that this world has been given a Gospel that most people don't believe, whether they are Christian or non-Christian, believer or unbeliever. A person who doesn't believe the Gospel has taken the wrong course in life and will miss out on God's blessings. But even many Christians will not partake of God's divine nature until they get to Heaven. Why? Because they refuse to surrender to the promises of God.

God gave you many precious promises. You surrender to these divine promises when you commit yourself to living your entire life in the atmosphere of faith. That means when your body is in pain, your mouth says you are healed. When your mind says you are a failure, you speak the Word that says greater is He who is in you than he who is in the world (1 John 4:4).

As First John 5:4 says, you overcome by your faith the circumstances you see with your natural eyes:

For whatever is born of God overcomes the world. And this is the victory that has overcome the world — our faith.

Does that mean God suddenly works a miracle in every situation you face? No, the outcome of any given situation is determined by the way you approach it.

Do you approach a problem with a fatalistic attitude that complains, "Oh, no, not again! Everything always goes wrong in my life! Everything is just so horrible. Every day I get up just to get knocked down all over again!" Or do you overcome the problem by speaking faith in God's promises until circumstances line up with His Word?

It's all in the way you perceive your life. Do you perceive life from the perspective that your cup is half empty or your cup is half full? Do you look at life from the viewpoint that says, "Look how far I still have to go" or "Look how far I've come"?

Anytime you're having a hard time believing the promises of God, you can know that your mind is being blinded by the god of this world. You may not even recognize that it's happening.

But think back to the time you first started walking by faith. No one could ever talk you out of a promise of God back then! You'd say, "All the promises in this Book are mine!" People may have thought you sounded silly, but I tell you what — you were victorious!

Reining in the Carnal Imagination

If you're experiencing problems maintaining the level of faith you once had for the exceedingly precious promises of God, the place you're having a difficult time is in your imagination.

"How do you know my problem is my imagination, Robb?"

The power of the imagination to affect what a person believes has been proven. For instance, I once read about two people who actually became paralyzed within a week of being told that the water they had been drinking was seriously contaminated. Yet in reality, there was nothing wrong with the water!

You see, there is great power in your "imaginator." It determines which way you look at a situation.

Ask yourself, *How am I viewing this situation? Am I looking at it with the attitude that I can take*

44

the devil, or am I expecting him to pound me to the ground?

Think about young David when he was faced with the giant Goliath. David never ran at Goliath until he found out there was a reward. You see, when you focus on the reward, you'll run toward Goliath to defeat him. When you focus on how big the giant is, you'll run from him. It's all in what you allow yourself to imagine.

Do you remember what God said concerning the people who built the tower of Babel?

And the Lord said, Behold, the people is one, and they have all one language; and this they begin to do: and now nothing will be restrained from them, which they have imagined to do.

Genesis 11:6 *KJV*

The principle God states in this verse can be extended to include this meaning: *If you can get what you think, what you believe, and what you say all on the same page, you can't be stopped.* On the other hand, the enemy can stop you every time when your thoughts and your words don't match what you believe.

Jesus emphasized this principle in Matthew 12:35,37:

"A good man out of the good treasure of his heart brings forth good things, and

an evil man out of the evil treasure brings forth evil things....
"For by your words you will be justified. And by your words you will be condemned."

You can see why it's so important to commit yourself to living your life in an atmosphere of faith as you surrender to the promises of God!

Applying All Diligence To Excellence

Now let's go back to Second Peter 1:4 (*KJV*) and see *why* God gives us His precious promises:

Whereby are given unto us exceeding great and precious promises: that by these ye might be partakers of the divine nature, having escaped the corruption that is in the world through lust.

God gives us His promises so we can escape the corruption of the world and the pressures that are placed on us every day. He does *not* give us His promises so we can pull one out of our little plastic, bread-loaf-shaped "promise box" each morning and say, "Okay, here's my promise for the day" — and then go about our daily routine without ever applying that promise to our lives!

It doesn't do us any good to be given divine promises if we walk away and forget what those promises are. That's why Peter said in verse 5 (*KJV*), **"And beside this, giving all diligence...."** That just means, "Focus on this. Stop breaking focus. Don't let yourself get sidetracked from God's promises."

Now let's go on to look at the steps you are to take to move up higher in God, which is the prerequisite to rising to the next level at your job. First, verse 5 (*KJV*) says, **"...Giving all diligence, add to your faith virtue...."** The word "virtue" here has that same meaning of *moral excellence*. You are to add moral excellence to your faith.

Now, you have probably already figured out that this process isn't as easy as it sounds. People talk about pursuing excellence all the time, but few accomplish it. I don't want that to describe me. I don't want to just talk about or hear about excellence — I want to *do* it. I'm determined to keep on stretching!

That's the stance you have to take in life to be a person of excellence. You can never live your life comfortably. You must always live out beyond your comfort zone — continuing to stretch in every area of your life, whether it's your love walk, your giving, or your role in the workplace.

So after you have realized that you have been given very great and exceedingly precious promises, your next step is to add to your faith virtue, or moral excellence. God is saying, "Don't just sit there and tell Me what you believe. I want to see your beliefs in action." In other words, *you are to add excellence to what you say you believe.*

47

This is what separates the men from the boys. Most people never get beyond this verse because they never turn their faith words into faith actions. They deceive themselves by saying, "Oh, I really do believe God." But if that is true, why are their lives in such a stinking mess?

So don't just sit around and *think* about what you believe. Get honest with yourself. If you haven't been acting on God's promises in your life, don't lie to yourself by claiming to believe them. Always remember:

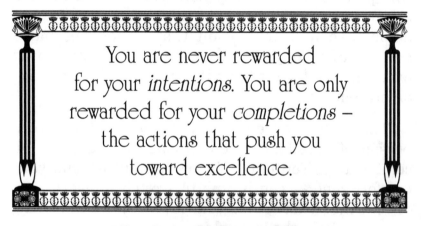

You are never rewarded for your *intentions*. You are only rewarded for your *completions* – the actions that push you toward excellence.

The Step-by-Step Climb
To the Next Level

Next, Peter provides the second step you must take on your way to another level: **"...Add to your faith virtue; and to virtue knowledge"** (v. 5 *KJV*).

Why is this the second step? Because after you have begun to live in excellence, you need knowledge in order to advance further.

48

This principle is certainly true in the arena of business. Someone once said to me, "You know, I love doing what I do for a living, but I just can't figure out the business end of it. Why doesn't God teach me about business?"

I responded, "Because God isn't a business teacher. God doesn't teach on business."

"Well, what should I do then?" the person asked.

"I can tell you what I would do. I'd sign up for a Dale Carnegie course on how to run a small business."

"But taking that course costs about two thousand dollars!"

"Yes," I countered, "but consider how much you're going to lose if you don't take a course like that to give you the knowledge you need to be successful in business."

One way or another, you can't escape from this principle. You simply cannot advance in any area of life without knowledge.

Peter then gives us the next step on the way to another level. He says in verse 6 (*KJV*) that we are to add **"...to knowledge, temperance...."**

Now, the word "temperance" can be replaced with the word "self-control." This makes a lot of sense when you think about it. You see, if we aren't able to control ourselves once we begin to advance further in our pursuit of excellence through knowledge, our flesh will want to get off the track and change locations! We'll need self-control just to hang in there when our emotions are saying, "I want off this train!"

The stakes are high at this stage in our walk with God. If we give up at that point, we will abort everything we've already accomplished, and we definitely don't want to do that!

Verse 6 (*KJV*) goes on to give you the next quality you are to add to your life in order to rise to another level: **"...and to temperance patience...."** That word "patience" is talking about *steadfastness* and *consistency*. This kind of godly consistency is a quality most people are missing in their lives.

Once again, consistency is referring to *focus*. When you add consistency to your life, you don't get turned to the right or to the left. You stay focused on God and your pursuit of living excellently before Him. You decide, "This is the time I pray every day. This is the time I get up in the morning to read the Word. This is the time I confess the Word. Before everything else crowds into my day, I will make sure I spend time with God!"

Peter then tells you the next thing you are to add to your life: **"...and to patience godliness"** (v.6 *KJV*). Why is this the next step? Because if you reach a place of consistency in your walk with God and you fail to add godliness to it, you'll become cocky. You'll think you know more than everyone else — that you have your act together, but everyone else is still waiting to get his or her act together.

You'll start thinking, *Oh, Lord, how long will I have to put up with these characters?*

So God tells you to add godliness to your life. That way you will walk in humility no matter what level you rise to in God.

What comes after godliness? Verse 7 (*KJV*) tells you: **"And to godliness brotherly kindness...."** It is possible to be godly and yet still act unkindly toward other people. But you *can* be kind to people because God tells you what to add to your kindness: **"...to brotherly kindness charity** [or God's kind of love]" (v. 7 *KJV*).

Yes, it is even possible to be kind without being loving! That's why love is such an important quality to add to your life. Indeed, each one of these ingredients are important for spiritual growth as you move on up to a new level in the workplace and in every other area of your life.

Fruitful or Spiritually Blind?

So what happens if you follow these steps that Peter has laid out for you? Verse 8 (*KJV*) spells it out:

For if these things be in you, and abound, they make you that ye shall neither be barren nor unfruitful in the knowledge of our Lord Jesus Christ.

This is quite a statement Peter has made! If these qualities he has talked about are inside you — if you are pressing toward them, pursuing them with all your strength — they will make you fruitful for the Kingdom of God in every arena of life, including your job!

So why is it that most Christians aren't fruitful? Because they don't keep pressing long enough to get beyond the initial excitement and cause these spiritual qualities to start working in their lives.

Then in verse 9 (*KJV*), Peter says something interesting: **"But he that lacketh these things is blind, and cannot see afar off...."** Why is this? Because if you refuse to go through this sequence, you put yourself at a great disadvantage. You begin to lose sight of what God has said about you:

- that you are righteous in Christ.

- that God has given you all things that pertain to life and godliness.

- that God has given you every character quality necessary for you to live a godly life.

- that the ability to be just like Jesus already resides down on the inside of you; you just need the knowledge and the moral excellence to bring it out and cause it to manifest in your life.

Once you begin to step up this ladder toward another level, don't ever let yourself take a step backwards. Remember, God said if you would walk up that ladder, you would never be unfruitful. He also said, "The one who lacks these things will become blind."

The person who refuses to walk up this ladder is the person who is losing his spiritual sight. He's beginning to degenerate in his spiritual ability to "see afar off" in life. Thus, he lets go of his desire to obtain God's long-term blessings and starts living for short-term gratification. He has forgotten this principle:

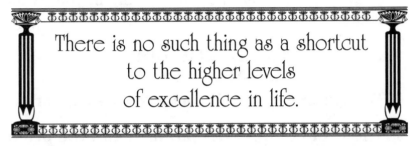

There is no such thing as a shortcut to the higher levels of excellence in life.

Because this person lacks the qualities to see with his spiritual eyes, he has also **"...forgotten that he was purged from his old sins"** (v. 9 *KJV*). All of a sudden, those sins start showing up again in his life. Things go from bad to worse as he begins to judge other people; meanwhile, he deceives himself into thinking he doesn't need to be forgiven anymore.

You don't ever want to put yourself in that position by refusing to take the steps God has given you for moving upward in Him. Keep yourself from slipping down the ladder that takes you to the next level. Make the decision, "As long as I live, I will never live for short-term gratification. Instead, I'll keep my eyes focused on my goal — to live excellently before God in the workplace and in every other area of my life!" That one decision will keep you from making a lot of stupid, unnecessary mistakes!

Friend, God has given you very great and exceedingly precious promises. It is by these promises that you can be a partaker of His divine nature. To this end, God didn't just give you *some* things to help you along the way; the Bible says He has given you *all* things that pertain to life and godliness. These are the truths you need to focus on as you pursue the next level of excellence at your job and in your walk with God!

PRINCIPLES FOR RISING TO ANOTHER LEVEL

★ **Today's excellence is tomorrow's mediocrity.**

★ **The proof of desire is *pursuit*, and the proof of pursuit is *favor*.**

★ **In order for you to obtain your goal, you must continually point your life in the direction of your desired destination.**

★ **Broken focus is the only reason for failure. Follow-through and completion is the only door to promotion.**

★ **The Excellent delight in the principles that will bring promotion.**

★ **The Excellent require God's Word to evaluate their own progress.**

★ **Sacrifice is the road traveled by the Excellent on their journey to their divine destiny.**

★ A Person of Excellence responds to God's commands with unquestioned obedience.

★ A Person of Excellence understands and embraces the power of the seed.

★ You are never rewarded for your *intentions*. You are only rewarded for your *completions* — the actions that push you toward excellence.

★ There is no such thing as a shortcut to the higher levels of excellence in life.

NOTES:

_____

_____

_____

_____

_____

_____

_____

_____

_____

_____

_____

NOTES:

CHAPTER TWO

HOW TO MULTIPLY YOUR LIFE INVESTMENT

You probably wouldn't be reading this book if you didn't have a desire to keep on moving upward in your profession. But you need to know more than just what steps to take in order to reach the next level. You also need to learn how to multiply what God has given you to invest in life so you can accelerate your growth in God, which in turn will accelerate your progress in the workplace.

You see, God created you to multiply because *He is a multiplier*. He doesn't divide. He doesn't subtract. Everything about Him either adds or multiplies.

The first commandment God ever gave to mankind was "Be fruitful and multiply" (Gen. 1:22). People think God was only talking about bearing children, but He wasn't. He was saying, "I'm a multiplier, so you must multiply as well."

You were born with a desire to multiply. That's why when you first start a new job, you come in with such high hopes of advancement and promotion.

That's how God created you to think because He wants you to multiply the gifts He has given you. He wants you to be all He intends for you to be.

Establishing Life Goals

It is my personal desire never to waste or squander a moment of this life God has given me. I want to invest my life in ways that will bring Him glory and that will give my loved ones and the future generations to come the greatest benefit.

If that is your desire as well, there are some questions you need to answer as you set out on your life course:

- *Where do I want to go in life?*

- *What has God called me to do with my life?*

- *What is it that I want to achieve in the days and years to come?*

- *What am I currently doing toward the fulfillment of my goals?*

Proverbs 13:4 (*KJV*) says, **"The soul of the sluggard desireth, and hath nothing: but the soul of the diligent shall be made fat."** Many people spend their entire lives desiring what they don't have. These same people usually find a way to blame others for their inability to get what they want.

But you can never rightfully blame others for not receiving the blessings promised in the Word. The

Bible says God will always make sure you are recompensed for obeying Him:

For God is not unjust to forget your work and labor of love which you have shown toward His name, in that you have ministered to the saints, and do minister.

Hebrews 6:10

God will owe no man anything. That means He will never allow a situation in which you are able to say you did what He asked you to do and never received the fruit of it.

The problem with most people who never achieve success in life is that they never set any goals for themselves. They don't know where they're going in life. They really don't want to go anywhere. They're just existing until tomorrow, thinking, *Maybe someone will discover how great I am one of these days!* But I can tell you right now, no one ever will.

People who fit in this category can live their entire lives without ever truly giving of themselves to others. They don't give themselves to their employer, to their friends — not even to their marriage partner. Instead, they always expect others to be the givers, while they remain continually in the role of receiver. No matter how much other people do for them, they are never satisfied because the real problem doesn't lie with others; it lies with their own refusal to give of themselves and to change what needs to be changed.

59

People like that are never going to prosper in life because the only way to activate the law of sowing and reaping is to be a sower. In Deuteronomy 30:19, Moses stood up before Israel and said, **"I call heaven and earth as witnesses today against you, that I have set before you life and death, blessing and cursing; therefore CHOOSE LIFE, that both you and your descendants may live."**

Moses was saying, "I'm setting this choice before you, and I'm calling Heaven and earth to record this day which way you choose."

You see, each time you choose life and blessing — each time you choose to give of yourself — you obligate the law of sowing and reaping to be to you what you were to someone else. That law has been programmed by God, so it must produce a harvest for the seed you sow.

A person who gives of himself in life is an influencer because giving is infectious. A person who gives influences every life he touches for the better.

However, most people live their lives taking much more than they ever give. Their lives can be likened to fluorescent lamps. This type of lamp performs a specific, limited function. It doesn't give off much light or heat. A person can't even read well by the light of one fluorescent lamp. That's why people don't use a lot of fluorescent lights to provide general lighting in their homes.

Now compare a fluorescent light to the lights used by camera crews when taping a television program. I guarantee you, it gets hot when I'm preaching a sermon for my television program under the intense glare of those lights! Much more intense even than these lights, however, is the beam of a laser light — a light that is so hot, it can cut through steel!

It's sad to say, but most Christians live their lives as fluorescent lamps. They just kind of "mosey" through life. They're not out to make any positive changes in their workplace or their community. The people who work around them may not even know who they are. These Christians will come and go, and people won't even care that they ever lived.

Then there are those "laser-beam" Christians. These are the people who begin to take steps up to the next level in life. They have decided to make a difference in this world. They're going to leave a mark on society that would not have been there if they hadn't been born.

You see, it's one thing for you to be a believer. It's another thing altogether to use the power God gave you when you made Jesus your Savior to change the world around you for His Kingdom. However, you can't change your world until you first allow God's power to change you.

According to what I've observed over the years, most Christians refuse to do much of anything about their faults and shortcomings. They want you to accept them just the way they are in their mediocre state and to forgive them just because you're a

Christian. That shows that they believe more in your Christianity than they believe in their own!

Think about it — why does so much of the world view Christianity as "a poor man's religion"? Why do so many successful people in the world say that Christianity is weak and that Christians don't have anything going for them? I'll tell you why — because too many Christians don't believe enough in anything to stand up for it. They don't really make a mark on society. They want to go to church sometimes, but they don't want anyone telling them that they need to move up higher and excel in their walk with God.

You know, I may not be real smart, but I'm smart enough to know that this life I'm living right now is coming to a close one day. With every breath I breathe, that's one breath closer to the end. That's why my investments into this natural life don't really matter to me. It's my investment into the life to come that truly matters.

So I'm not going to wait until I'm old and sitting in my rocking chair before I tell my grandchildren that they need to go to church and pray or that they need to be people of integrity who keep their word. I'm going to live my life that way now before those grandchildren are ever born so I can speak into their lives from their earliest memories. If I'd had someone to speak into my life like that when I was young, it would have made the early days of my Christian experience so much easier.

You see, God isn't looking for people to make it on their own personality. He's looking for those who will learn how to multiply the gifts and talents He has given them through investment, just as the two faithful servants did in Jesus' parable of the talents (Matt. 25:14-30).

Point Your Life In the Right Direction

So how do you multiply your seed in the workplace? How do you accelerate your growth through wise investment of that which God has given you? The first thing you have to do is *figure out what you are good at.* What skills or talents do you possess? What do you most like to do?

One clue to help you discover what you're called to solve in life can be found by determining what angers you. Personally, one of the things that angers me most is mediocrity. When I see a person doing nothing with his life, that makes me angry! I think, *Man, you're just taking up precious air! Someone else could take your place and do something with his life!*

Remember, I told you earlier that excellence is my passion. So if a person comes to my church and wants to stay mediocre, I can guarantee you this: Eventually I'm going to make that person angry. It might take two weeks, a month, or a year. (Some people who want to stay mediocre have even lasted five or ten years!) But sooner or later, that person will get upset and want to leave the church, and I'll be the reason.

You see, God didn't call me to be that person's friend; He called me to light a fire under him. I want him to feel the heat of godly conviction everywhere he goes as he thinks about what I've said.

I know I'm on a divine mission to eradicate mediocrity and instill an unending desire for excellence in the life of every person I minister to. In the same way, you need to find your divine mission and then point your life in the direction of *your* God-ordained goals.

Get Rid of the 'Extra Weights'

What is the second thing you must do to multiply your life investment and accelerate your growth in fulfilling God's call on your life? Romans 12:1,2 has the answer: You are to present yourself as a living sacrifice unto the Lord.

I beseech you therefore, brethren, by the mercies of God, that you present your bodies a living sacrifice, holy, acceptable to God, which is your reasonable service.
And do not be conformed to this world, but be transformed by the renewing of your mind, that you may prove what is that good and acceptable and perfect will of God.

When you are born again, God cleans out everything on the inside of you and makes you a new creation in Christ. The only problem you have now is your brain. That's why the Bible tells you to present yourself as a living sacrifice so you can be transformed by the renewing of your mind.

As you renew your mind with the Word, you'll discover some things over the course of time that you need to cut out of your life. You see, your "rocket" can't launch off its pad to the next level in life if you don't get rid of the extra weight that holds it down. Hebrews 12:1 talks about this principle:

Therefore we also, since we are surrounded by so great a cloud of witnesses, let us lay aside every weight, and the sin which so easily ensnares us, and let us run with endurance the race that is set before us.

Now, some of these "extra weights" may even seem good in themselves. But if they hold you back in any way from multiplying that which God has given you for His purposes in your life, those "good" things may need to go. The apostle Paul, who was a master at multiplying his own God-given investments, said it like this:

All things are lawful for me, but all things are not helpful. All things are lawful for me, but I will not be brought under the power of any.

1 Corinthians 6:12

All things are lawful, but not all things are profitable. All things are lawful, but not all things edify.

1 Corinthians 10:23 *NAS*

More than likely, you have things in your life you need to eliminate in order to become all God wants you to be. These things could include hobbies, interests, activities, or other time commitments that, in themselves, are good but are hindering you from moving up to the next level. At work, you might be wasting too much time with coworker conversations or low-priority tasks.

I recommend that you take the time to prayerfully evaluate your life. Is anything harming your effectiveness in fulfilling what God has called you to do? If so, you need to eliminate that hindrance from your life.

Now, I realize that it's easier to get rid of your old sins and bad habits than it is to eliminate the good things that need to go. Your mind may fight this whole idea, wondering, *But why would I want to eliminate good things from my life?*

I'll tell you why:

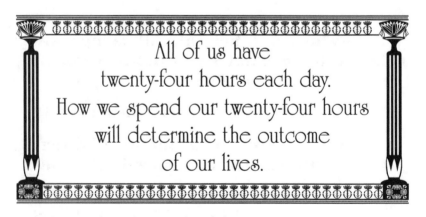

All of us have
twenty-four hours each day.
How we spend our twenty-four hours
will determine the outcome
of our lives.

You can't do everything, friend; you only have twenty-four hours in a day. Therefore, you need to ask yourself, *What's my top priority?*

Your top priority should be God. Everything in your life should revolve around Him, and that includes your vocation. What you do for a living or in ministry comes after God in your life — not before Him, not around Him, but *after* Him.

Most people make excuses about their messed-up priorities, saying, "Well, I can't spend time with God because I have to feed my family." But if these people don't get their priorities straight and put God at the top of their list, their family isn't going to get fed. Instead, they will keep pouring their money into a bag that has holes in it!

So cut out any habit, relationship, interest, or activity that hinders you from putting God first or from becoming productive at your job. If you're going to multiply what God has invested in you, you can't hold on to anything that subtracts or divides!

Don't Lose Focus

Proverbs 29:18 (*KJV*) is a familiar verse that says, **"Where there is no vision, the people perish...."** This proverb is talking about the result of losing focus. That's why it's so important that you get hindrances out of your life that cause you to break your focus.

But notice what this proverb says: Without a vision, people perish. Let me tell you about this word "perish." It could also be translated this way:

- "Without a vision, people *go backwards.*"

- "Without a vision, people *go without.*"

67

- "Without a vision, people *go naked.*"

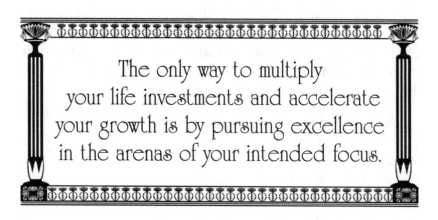

The only way to multiply your life investments and accelerate your growth is by pursuing excellence in the arenas of your intended focus.

Too many Christians are going backwards instead of forward in life. Perhaps they stopped focusing on God and His purposes for their lives. Instead of excelling in their God-ordained arenas of focus, they have just been existing, and they know it.

Does this sound familiar? Well, it's time to catch the vision of what God has called you to pursue in life! Remember the questions you have to ask yourself:

- *Where do I want to go in life?*

- *What has God called me to do with my life?*

- *What is it that I want to achieve in the days and years to come?*

- *What am I currently doing toward the fulfillment of my goals?*

Respect:
The Prerequisite for Promotion

One of the qualities that brings the greatest return on any investment in the workplace and in other areas of your life is *respect*. This is the reason:

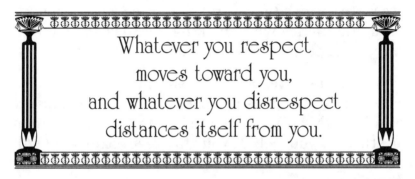

Whatever you respect
moves toward you,
and whatever you disrespect
distances itself from you.

For instance, if you don't understand or respect your finances, money will leave you. You may earn a lot of money, but you'll never be able to accumulate it. On the other hand, if you both understand and respect the value of money, it will come toward you and overtake your life.

This is true in any arena of life and in any relationship. If you act disrespectfully or indifferently toward a person, that person will distance himself from you and ultimately exit from your life.

Just take the case of marriage partners. A spouse who isn't respected may not leave the marriage physically, but he or she will certainly become emotionally distant from the one who is acting disrespectfully. On the other hand, marriage partners who show respect to each other find themselves increasingly drawn closer to each other through the years.

You see, intimacy doesn't necessarily guarantee access to a person, but respect does. Just read the book of Esther, and you'll see what I mean. Queen Vashti was closest to the king in relationship. But because she showed disrespect by refusing to come to him when he requested her presence, she lost her access to him. By contrast, Esther succeeded in gaining audience with the king because she showed him the respect due his office.

This issue of respect makes a huge difference in the workplace because *respect guarantees access*. It doesn't matter if you seem to be "on the short end of the stick" at your job. If you stay respectful, God will turn that stick around!

An employer is almost always willing to listen to an employee who never shows anything but respect when he talks to his boss about different matters. That's the kind of employee an employer will listen to all day long!

You can see this quality in the Proverbs 31 woman. Proverbs 31:26 says this woman **"...opens her mouth with wisdom, and on her tongue is the law of kindness."** Do you want to know how to get your employer's attention? Always speak quietly with respect and with kindness. It isn't so much *what* you say to him, but *how* you say it.

Most people don't realize that the quality of their work doesn't necessarily get them noticed on the job. Ultimately, it is respect that will get a person noticed and promoted; then it is the quality of that person's work that *keeps* him on that higher level.

I personally know many people who work hard at their job but are disrespectful toward their boss. Then they wonder why the boss never seems to notice them when it comes time for promotion. But I know exactly why. It is their disrespect that is keeping them from being promoted. You see, disrespect divides rather than multiplies any investment a person has made at his job because an employer can't put disrespect in a position of authority. If he did, the eventual result would be anarchy in the workplace.

Over the years, I have observed that disrespectful people are usually either angry or afraid. First, they may be angry that no one has discovered their worthiness to be placed in a position of authority. They refuse to admit that they may not have been "discovered" yet because they're not ready to be discovered!

Second, a disrespectful person may be afraid that he will be taken advantage of if he yields to someone else's way of doing things. The root of this fear is a lack of trust in God. In other words, the person doesn't trust God's wisdom regarding whom He has placed over him in authority.

This kind of situation is a tragedy, because the loss of respect is the reason so many people have come as far as they're ever going to go in their vocation. No matter what level a person is at in the workplace, respect is one thing God requires if that person wants to be promoted to the next level.

In fact, there are two verses in the book of Proverbs that promise great rewards of multiplication and promotion to those who are respectful and pure of heart:

He who loves purity of heart and has grace on his lips, the king will be his friend.

Proverbs 22:11

Do you see a man who excels in his work? He will stand before kings; he will not stand before unknown men.

Proverbs 22:29

The person who excels at being pure of heart and who always speaks respectful words of grace in the workplace will not remain in the background. God will continue to promote him to positions of greater responsibility until one day he stands before kings. In other words, he will find supernatural favor with those in the highest positions of honor and influence!

'What Part Do I Play In This Relationship?'

Many times your level of respect is dependent on your ability to recognize who you are in any given relationship. You have to be able to accurately answer the question, *What part do I play in the relationship I am in with this person?*

This explains why Jesus' natural brothers and sisters didn't ever walk with Him during His lifetime on this earth. They didn't respect Him. You see, whatever is close to a person often becomes invisible to him. Jesus said it like this: **"...A prophet is not without honor except in his own country and in his own house"** (Matt. 13:57). That means some of the greatest problems Jesus ever faced in His life were in His own house — with His own brothers and sisters and with His own mother.

"Oh, no," you may protest, "I believe Jesus' mother Mary was really nice!"

Yet Mary was the one standing outside when Jesus turned around and asked, "Who is My mother, and who are My brothers? Those who hear the Word and do it are My mother and sisters and brothers" (*see* Matt. 12:48-50). Jesus' words suggest that it may have taken years for Mary to truly understand who she was in her relationship with her Son Jesus.

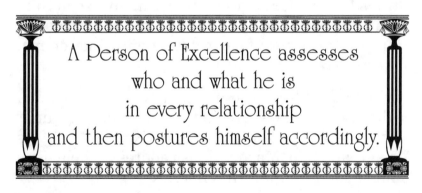

A Person of Excellence assesses
who and what he is
in every relationship
and then postures himself accordingly.

Whether or not a person recognizes who he is in his relationships will determine his outcome in life. For instance, I am the pastor at my church, and my church staff works under me. The staff members have to respect the position of authority I stand in, even if they don't respect me as a person.

73

"Well, yes, but what happens if you do a poor job of exercising your authority?"

What does that have to do with it? And who decides whether or not I'm doing a good job? Those who are supposed to respect me as their authority? That isn't the way it works, friend. They're not supposed to be focusing on my performance; they're supposed to be concentrating on whether or not they are being good employees for me!

The truth is, most of the employers in America are begging good people to come to work. All a person needs to do is go to work, do a good job, and respect his superiors. If an employer thinks he has found someone he can trust, that person will have himself a promotion in the first week! Employers are always looking for someone they can give something to, and every employee they find has learned to multiply his or her life investment with one common quality — *respect.*

When I address those whom God has placed in authority over me — even if they are much my junior in age — I say, "Yes, Sir" and "No, Sir" or "Yes, Ma'am" and "No, Ma'am." I also address people using "Mister" or "Mrs." all the time.

"Oh, no, he's just Bob."

Not to me, he isn't. He may be Bob to you, but he is "Sir" or "Mister So-and-so" to me! To those who are over me in authority, I say, "Yes, Sir. Whatever you like, Sir. How would you like it done? What do you think about that?" I don't say, "Well, I think you're wrong about this." You see, I have to recognize who I am in every relationship.

God is the One who sets the parameters for all your relationships. Paul understood this fact well, as we see in Acts 23 when he was brought before the Jewish council:

Then Paul, looking earnestly at the council, said, "Men and brethren, I have lived in all good conscience before God until this day."

And the high priest Ananias commanded those who stood by him to strike him on the mouth.

Then Paul said to him, "God will strike you, you whitewashed wall! For you sit to judge me according to the law, and do you command me to be struck contrary to the law?"

And those who stood by said, "Do you revile God's high priest?"

Then Paul said, "I did not know, brethren, that he was the high priest; for it is written, 'You shall not speak evil of a ruler of your people.'"

Acts 23:1-5

The high priest ordered Paul to be hit in the face, and Paul's first reaction was to rebuke him for his unjust command. Then those around Paul asked, "Do you understand that he is the high priest?"

Paul immediately backed down and said, "No, I didn't know that." Then he referred to God's Law as his standard for relating to the high priest of his people: **"...For it is written, 'You shall not speak evil of a ruler of your people'"** (v. 5).

It should be the same way in your life. God's Word is to determine your actions within each of your relationships with other people. If you are an employer, God has set down the parameters of your relationship with your employees. If you are an employee, He has set down the parameters of your relationship with your employer. It doesn't matter where you work; God's framework is still the same, and it is based entirely upon *respect*.

Now, it's important to understand that you don't necessarily respect the person, but you always respect the position that person holds. In other words, you respect *through* the person to God.

I respect God in the midst of every situation I face. The person standing in front of me might be acting like he doesn't deserve one ounce of respect. But that doesn't matter to me; I'm going to show respect for him because I'm respecting God *through* him. I can just look through that person and smile because I know Heaven is multiplying my reward back to me.

This is what Jesus did when He stood before the high priest and was unjustly condemned. First Peter 2:23 (*KJV*) says, **"...When he was reviled, reviled not again; when he suffered, he threatened not;**

but committed himself to him that judgeth righteously."

The Meaning of 'Respect'

Respect is a very interesting word. Society has spent the last forty years dismantling the meaning of the word "respect." As a result, many people don't even know what this word means. They don't respect themselves, let alone someone else! Nonetheless, respect is a powerful force, absolutely essential for multiplying your life investment within the workplace.

So let's talk about the meaning of the word "respect." In part, it means *giving attention to*. Respect also carries the meaning of *holding others in high esteem* or *deeming others as distinguished and worthy*.

Think about it — whom do you hold in high esteem? Whom do you give your attention to? What position of worth do you allow the people God has placed in your life to occupy?

You see, one thing people don't usually do for others is give them their undivided attention. Most people already know in their own minds what they think about a given subject. Therefore, they often don't show other people respect by giving attention to what they have to say.

I don't want my employees to give attention to what other ministers think about the dynamics of working in this church. What other ministers think about what goes on within these church walls really doesn't matter to me. They have no authority over this church because they are not responsible for it.

Often the reason other employers look better to an employee than his own employer is that he doesn't have to submit to those other employers. The employee might say, "I just love the way that person runs his business!" — not realizing how difficult it is to work under the tough standards of that particular employer. For instance, one employer I know doesn't tolerate even one negative word coming out of his employees' mouths. If someone starts criticizing or complaining, that person is fired on the spot.

I'm telling you, it's just better for you to hold in high esteem and give attention to those whom God has placed in authority over *you*!

Respect is also a quality that lives on the inside of a person. The truth is, all life is lived from the internal rather than from the external. In fact, I'll go so far as to say this: *The way a person looks on the outside is the way he lives on the inside.*

All you need to do is look at the inside of your car if you want to find out how you're doing on the inside of *you*. If you have a mold farm growing on some five-month-old french fries stuck beneath the front seat, that's a good indication that you need to make some changes!

I know what I'm talking about because of the way I was raised. The unkempt condition of our home was only a reflection of the chaos and turmoil that lived on the inside of each of us in my family.

As a young boy, I would know my mom was drinking if I opened the front door of our house and found myself suddenly ankle-deep in newspapers, dirt, and junk scattered all over the floor. If I ever wanted to find something to wear, I had to find it in the pile of clothes that always lay on the floor. Nothing was ever hung in a closet.

The disorder on the inside of my parents became the way our entire family lived our lives on the outside. I'm so grateful to God that, years later, both my parents gave their lives to Jesus and were changed from the inside out!

Because respect is an inward quality, no one can make someone into a respectful person. A person is respectful because he *chooses* to be respectful.

You see, people cannot earn respect. They may earn others' *adherence* or *false loyalty*, but they don't earn their *respect*. Respect is given; loyalty is earned. Respect is the quality originating in a person's mind, the course of action from which proceeds that person's esteem for others. It involves giving due attention and showing favor to another.

In the case of Cain and his brother Abel, both men brought the Lord an offering. The Bible says that God gave attention or had respect unto Abel and his offering, but unto Cain and his offering God did not have respect (Gen. 4:4,5).

You see, God looks on the inside, at the heart of man. He respected Abel's heart and, therefore, his offering because Abel did what he knew was right.

But God did not respect Cain's heart; therefore, He didn't respect or give attention to Cain's offering.

Don't Correct Upwards

People don't realize how much they subtract from their position in the workplace when they refuse to respect. A person who lives in disrespect is at the height of his game already; he will never go further in his vocation. His employer can't trust him because he's always voicing his own opinions and criticizing the way his employer does things.

That kind of disrespectful behavior inevitably causes the employer to become angry and edgy with the employee. The only antidote to this situation is found in Proverbs 15:1: **"A soft answer turns away wrath...."** In other words, to change the relationship with his employer and get rid of the anger, that employee needs to become "soft" and respectful in the way he talks *to* his employer and *about* his employer to others.

Now, the employee might protest, "Yes, but my employer shouldn't be like that!" or "He's dealing with that situation all wrong!" I'm not saying an employer is always right in the way he carries out his responsibilities. But it isn't his employees' job to tell him that he's wrong!

Let me tell you how to avoid this pitfall of disrespect:

80

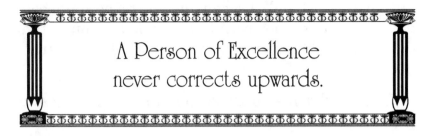

A Person of Excellence never corrects upwards.

God never called us to correct our superiors. Now, our superiors may learn something from us; they may even receive a tremendous amount of wisdom from us. But God never called us to correct them. Correction at the job or anywhere else in life comes from *above*, never from *beneath*.

The moment we make the authority figures God has placed in our lives become our rivals or our equals — the moment their opinions don't mean very much to us — is the moment they cease to be whom God has called them to be in our lives. At that point, our employers can no longer teach us, for we have changed the parameters of the relationship.

Also, we need to understand this: When we begin to make allegiances with people who are in disagreement with our authorities in the workplace, we are actually taking steps toward the enemy and causing our authorities to take steps *away* from us.

Suddenly our superiors start looking at us to see if our words match our actions. They are no longer sure they can trust us, for we have begun to allow mingled seed to be planted in our minds. We're hearing information from two directions — from our authorities and from those who are criticizing our authorities — and it's causing us to become both disloyal and disrespectful. If we keep going that direction, we'll never become what God wants us to become.

That's why it's so important to understand this principle:

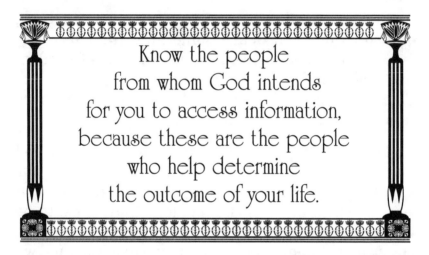

Know the people
from whom God intends
for you to access information,
because these are the people
who help determine
the outcome of your life.

There are essentially two kinds of people in your life — those who always want to make you comfortable, and those who are in your life for change. The first group of people doesn't spur you on. They don't cause you to change. They don't urge you to become better. That's why you gravitate toward this kind of person when you are content with staying in the mediocrity of your comfort zone.

The latter group of people are usually the authorities God has placed over you in the various arenas of life, including your employer at work. With these people, you may continually feel a certain pressure to change, to grow, to become better, to move on to the next level.

But that is a healthy type of pressure, needed in your life to help you become all God intends for you to be. If you turn away from these people — the ones God has ordained that you access information from — and become a companion of those who are disloyal and devoid of respect, the Bible says you will suffer the consequences:

He who walks with wise men will be wise, but the companion of fools will be destroyed.

Proverbs 13:20

Throughout my years of ministry, I've seen this principle in operation in the workplace so many times. You just can't make strange bedfellows with discontented, disrespectful coworkers and get away with it. Those people may harbor hidden motives that you'll never understand. You really don't know why they became your friend. It's possible they did it just so they could undermine your position.

We just need to get it out of our minds that we have the right to correct someone above us in authority, because we don't. In order to accelerate our growth in the workplace, we must give up what the world calls our "rights." Otherwise, we won't be able to move up to the fullness of God's will for us at our jobs.

You may ask, "What happens if the situation at my job is way out of kilter?" That's when you better lay prostrate on the floor, throw yourself on the mercy of the heavenly court, and pray, "God, I need Your mercy. I need Your love and forgiveness. And I need a good dose of Your longsuffering with this supervisor of mine, Lord. Help him, Jesus. But if he isn't going to let You fix him, then please move him on up. Promote him to another position so he can be blessed and I can work in peace!"

Don't Take Your Employer for Granted

Here is another principle you need to understand in order to avoid paying the penalties that result from disrespect on the job:

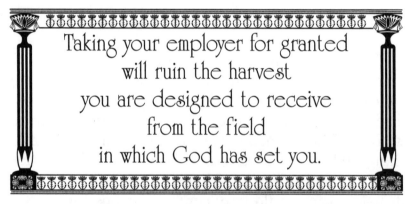

Taking your employer for granted will ruin the harvest you are designed to receive from the field in which God has set you.

Over-familiarity is often the culprit that causes us to take our authorities for granted and overstep our bounds with them. When that happens, our employers can no longer be in our lives what God has called them to be. *Remember, whatever or whomever becomes familiar to us becomes hidden to us.*

Whenever we go beyond our authority's invitation to intimacy, this reproach of familiarity will attempt to invade our lives. It's a sin we don't talk much about, for it's very subtle. Gradually we become too familiar with the individuals God has placed over us in life. As a result, we don't realize what we have in these people until they have exited our lives.

So keep this principle in mind at all times:

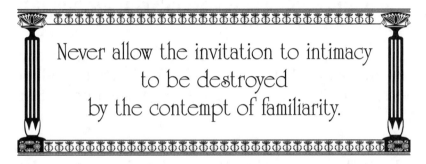

Never allow the invitation to intimacy
to be destroyed
by the contempt of familiarity.

Remember — just because your employer invites you to a greater level of intimacy with him doesn't mean you have been invited to have an opinion about the way he conducts himself in his overseeing responsibilities.

This leads to another principle of respect to abide by in the workplace:

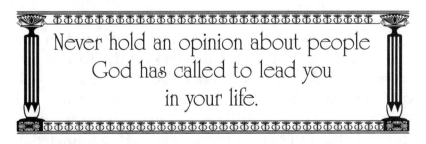

Never hold an opinion about people
God has called to lead you
in your life.

That includes, of course, our superiors at our place of employment. We must also learn not to see or hear others who voice their negative opinions about these authority figures.

We may never understand why our authorities do what they do or say what they say. But that isn't our business anyway. As David says in Psalm 139:6, there are some things we aren't supposed to know: **"Such knowledge is too wonderful for me; it is high, I cannot attain it."**

We are to stay out of the business of those who are above us. God hasn't called us to that level, so we shouldn't even try to go there. We cannot attain to it.

Job said it like this: **"You asked, 'Who is this who hides counsel without knowledge?'..."** (Job 42:3). You see, it takes knowledge to hide counsel. People can actually become schizophrenic if their minds can't handle the knowledge they have received. For instance, when children see and experience sexual intimacy too early in their lives, they often can't handle the knowledge they have received and therefore try to subconsciously hide it. This can affect them so profoundly mentally and emotionally that they never recover.

Verse 3 goes on to say, **"...Therefore I have uttered what I did not understand, things too wonderful for me, which I did not know."** Job was saying, "I started talking about things I shouldn't have been talking about. I thought about things I shouldn't be thinking about. It is knowledge that is too high for me. I'm not at that level yet. God, forgive me for getting involved in things I shouldn't be involved in."

This is the same mistake many people make in the workplace. They get their mouths and their thoughts involved in matters they shouldn't be tampering with.

"But I don't agree with what my employer is doing!" they say. But what difference does it make whether or not they agree with their employer? God hasn't called them to fill that position, so they have no right to voice an opinion!

For many years, this has been a guideline I follow at the workplace: Whoever the authority is, I always agree with him.

"Yes, but what if he does something wrong?"

Well, if it has to do with the job, I wouldn't know about any mistake my superior made because I haven't been released to the level of security that he occupies. That means I will never know if he is doing something wrong. I'm just here to please him.

I guarantee you this: If you take this position with your superiors in the workplace, it will quickly convince you that you can't have an opinion about them! You'll stop trying to make decisions that are not your responsibility to make.

That was King Saul's mistake (*see* 1 Samuel 15). He allowed the pressure of the people to put him in a position where he made a decision contrary to his authority — God Himself. God had commanded him

87

to utterly destroy the Amalekites, taking no captives alive or any of the spoils gained from his victory over them. But Saul decided to take captive the Amalekite king, as well as the best of the livestock to sacrifice to the Lord.

When the prophet Samuel saw what he had done, he said to Saul, **"...When you were little in your own eyes, were you not head of the tribes of Israel? And did not the Lord anoint you king over Israel?"** (v. 17). In other words, Samuel was saying, "You used to be humble before the Lord and small in your own eyes. But when you made decisions today that you shouldn't have made, you took a position God never gave you."

In verse 28, Samuel told Saul the dire consequences of his disrespect and rebellion toward the Lord:

> **So Samuel said to him, "The Lord has torn the kingdom of Israel from you today, and has given it to a neighbor of yours, who is better than you."**

I don't know about you, but this passage of Scripture makes me want to stay continually small in my own eyes. I don't want to lose all I've invested into the call God has placed on my life!

Don't Question Your Authority

One reason respect brings such good returns on your life investment is that it helps keep your relationships with your authorities intact. That's a goal many people fail to reach. They can start relationships, but very few know how to keep those relationships going.

So let me tell you an important principle that will help you maintain a good relationship with your authority at work:

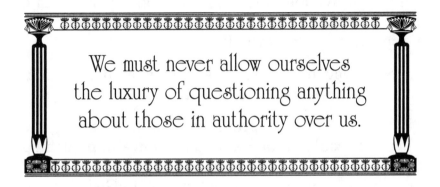

We must never allow ourselves the luxury of questioning anything about those in authority over us.

Time is a great tattletale; time will tell whether or not your employer is right. You don't even need to think about it. Remember, his job is not to answer to you. You don't work for the Holy Spirit, so you never need to check up on him. And why should you care what he says or thinks anyway? Promotion doesn't come from your employer; the Bible says that promotion comes from *the Lord*:

For promotion cometh neither from the east, nor from the west, nor from the south.
But God is the judge: he putteth down one, and setteth up another.

Psalm 75:6,7 *KJV*

I'll never forget the day a minister who was my authority got upset with me and said, "I'm going to 'blackball' you. You will never preach again for the rest of your life."

As the man kept raving on, I stopped him and said, "Forgive me, Sir. If you tell me never to stand up in front of a group of people and preach the Gospel again, I never will. "

Now, you may say, "Yes, but what if that man had told you never to preach again?"

I wouldn't have preached again. However, he obviously couldn't do that because I'm still preaching the Gospel today all over the world! You see, I wasn't trusting in that man; I was trusting in God *through* that man.

It all depends on how much you're going to trust God, friend. If you've decided to trust Him, then do it. Don't just pretend like you're trusting Him. Be who you are supposed to be in your relationship with your authorities at the job; then trust God to make every wrong situation right and to promote you in due time.

When you trust God like this and concentrate on staying respectful in the workplace, you'll be able to avoid all arguments with your superior. How is that possible? Because there is never a time when it's your place to challenge or complain about him. If you think you can give your employer his job description, why aren't you the employer? I'll tell you why — because God didn't call you to *be* the employer; He called you to *respect* the employer.

I assure you, complaining about your superior is *not* the way to multiply your assets at work and get promoted. God isn't going to say, "Wow, thanks for telling Me how bad your supervisor is! Since he isn't doing a good job, I'll make *you* the supervisor now!"

God doesn't want to hear anything negative coming out of your mouth because He knows you're doing nothing but sowing bad seed into your life. He knows that any complaints or criticisms that come out of your mouth are going to come back one day to smack you in the face and take away all you've gained thus far.

So if you don't like the way your employer runs things at the job, don't question his ability to carry out his authority. Instead, ask yourself this important question: *Am I being the employee I should be?* I guarantee that you'll have plenty to keep you busy as you honestly seek the answer to that question!

When Your Employer Is a Believer

One thing I've seen again and again in my years of ministry is the great number of Christian employees who believe it is God's will for them to be critical of their Christian employers. They think, *Since my employer and I are both Christians, that gives me the right to criticize the way he runs things.*

For some reason, these Christian employees have the idea that they can say whatever they want to say to their employer. They also think they have the right to come in late. They even get upset and consider it an imposition if their employer asks them why they didn't arrive to work on time! It is absolutely unnerving to me to see how ungrateful these Christians are for what their employers have done for them.

No matter what our employer has ever said or done, nothing gives us the right to be critical of him or her. We never have the right to be critical of an employer, Christian or non-Christian.

You may ask, "Why would Christians act so disrespectfully toward their Christian employers?" It's real simple. They don't understand this principle of servanthood:

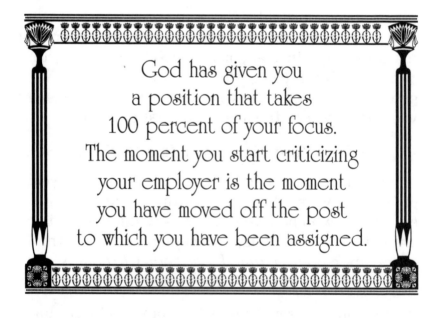

God has given you
a position that takes
100 percent of your focus.
The moment you start criticizing
your employer is the moment
you have moved off the post
to which you have been assigned.

When you work for a Christian employer, you need to be the very best employee that your

92

employer has ever had. You must work as a servant, not as a judge, with the motivation not of making money, but of making your employer and that business very prosperous. As you do this, God will see that you prosper as well.

It's amazing to me how many Christian employees are able to tell me exactly what their employers are doing wrong. As they talk, I think, *Wait a minute! If you are so smart, why isn't YOUR name on the sign in front of your employer's office? Did you ever think for a moment that maybe you weren't the person God wanted to be in charge for a reason? If you "had the goods" to be the one in authority, God would make sure you WERE in authority!*

When a person is put in charge of a company or business, he develops a whole new perspective on everything. Once he's in charge, he isn't as opinionated as he used to be because being the one in authority has a way of making a person more humble. Suddenly that person figures out that there is more than one way to skin a cat. In other words, he recognizes that he won't necessarily be making *right* decisions; he will be trying to make the *best* decisions he can.

The Bible is clear: If you are an employee, you must see your superior at work as deserving respect: otherwise, it will be a scandal to the Name of Christ:

All who are under the yoke of slavery should consider their masters worthy of full respect, so that God's name and our teaching may not be slandered.

Those who have believing masters are not to show less respect for them because they are brothers. Instead, they are to serve them even better, because those who benefit from their service are believers, and dear to them....

1 Timothy 6:1,2 *NIV*

We are never to take advantage of an employer just because he's our brother in the Lord. We shouldn't take even one moment of liberty with him because he is a Christian.

Actually, we should be doing the very opposite of that. We should be taking our personal time to serve him just because we want to! He's paying us to go one mile, but we can choose to go with him two miles because we are serving as unto God.

It's a whole new way of thinking, isn't it? But we are the only ones who can decide whether we are going to walk in respect or disrespect toward our Christian employer.

Long ago when I worked for that parcel delivery company, I made the decision that any of my supervisors' slightest wish would be my greatest command. Whenever they opened their mouths with a request, I would do my best to fulfill that request for them. One of my superiors made fun of me for that decision. He laughed at me and said, "Thompson, I'm going to bury you with work."

I said, "Excuse me, Sir, but you don't have enough work here to bury me. Whatever you'd like me to do, I'd be happy to do for you. That's why I'm here, Sir. I'm here to get you a promotion. I'm here to make money for you. I'm not here to take anything from you. I'm here to *give* you something."

Some of my supervisors may not have liked me and my stand for Jesus, but none of them could control me. How could they control a man who would give them more than they even had the guts to demand? What bothered them more than anything else was that they could never make me angry.

Other Christians who worked with me used to get absolutely irate about the way some of the supervisors would treat me. But I'd say, "It's all right, brothers. We are to serve them all the more. We're here to serve. We're here to bless. We're here to *give* to them, not *take* from them."

So I want to encourage you, friend — if you have a Christian employer, consider him worthy of full honor and respect so the Name of Jesus won't be slandered in your workplace. Choose God's way of respect, and be blessed!

Biblical Examples of Respect
And Disrespect

Let's look at a few biblical examples of people who either passed or failed the test of questioning their authorities' integrity, their motives, or their ability to lead. First, we find in Numbers 12 that Miriam and Aaron began to question Moses.

What happened to Miriam and Aaron? Miriam actually received her harvest from that bad seed right away. She contracted leprosy and had to be put out of the Israelite camp for seven days before the Lord restored her to health (vv. 10-15). Aaron reaped his harvest later when he went up on Mount Hor at the Lord's command and died there, never to set eyes on the Promised Land (Num. 33:38; Deut. 32:50).

Another example of a person who questioned the authority of his leader is found in Numbers 16. This man's name was Korah, one of the tribal leaders of Israel. Korah didn't respect Moses' and Aaron's authority, so he gathered some men around him for support and then challenged them both:

"...You take too much upon yourselves, for all the congregation is holy, every one of them, and the Lord is among them. Why then do you exalt yourselves above the assembly of the Lord?"

Numbers 16:3

Immediately Moses hit the deck because he knew how seriously the Lord views disrespect. Korah had not only questioned his authorities himself; he had led others into rebellion and had attempted to bring division among God's people. The consequences for Korah's actions were swift: The next day, the earth divided and swallowed not only him and everything that belonged to him, but all those who had participated in his rebellion (vv. 31-33)!

So what is the payoff for being respectful and refusing to question your authority? We can find the payoff of multiplication in the life of Joshua. First, we see in Numbers 13 and 14 that Joshua was a man of faith and integrity. He was one of the twelve spies Moses sent to spy out the Promised Land.

Now, you need to understand that Moses didn't send out ten stupid men and two smart men. He sent out the best man from every tribe. He wanted to know what the best of the best thought of the land God had promised them.

Nevertheless, ten of the twelve spies came back and said, "We can't do it. The giants are too big." But Joshua and Caleb, Moses' number-one and number-two students, said, "Moses, we can do this. Come on, men, God said we can do it, so we can!"

Through the years, Joshua remained a respectful, faithful man under Moses' leadership. As a result, God later chose him to be Moses' successor.

Now, we know that Moses wasn't a perfect leader. He made some mistakes along the way, and Joshua knew it. But later, after Joshua had taken over the leadership of the Israelites, the younger man spoke only words of honor and respect concerning his former leader.

For instance, Joshua said these words to the Israelites in Joshua 1:13: **"Remember the word which Moses the servant of the Lord commanded you...."** Notice that Joshua *didn't* say, "Boy, Moses made some big mistakes. Remember when he got angry and hit that rock to make water come out? He didn't even make it to the Promised Land! I'll tell

97

you what — Moses was really wrong in the way he handled some things."

No, Joshua didn't do that. He called his former leader *the servant of the Lord*.

You see, the quality of the student will always come out when the teacher makes a mistake. A respectful student realizes that he doesn't stop being a student, nor does he suddenly have the right to question his teacher's authority, just because his teacher does something wrong.

This leads to another principle of respect:

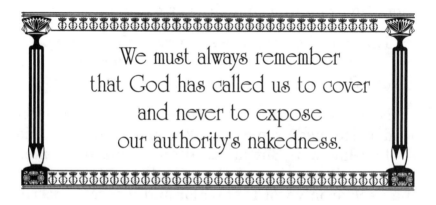

We must always remember that God has called us to cover and never to expose our authority's nakedness.

What do I mean by that? Well, let me take you to an account of Noah and his sons in Genesis 9:20-27 to show you what I mean.

After leaving the ark, Noah became a husbandman and planted a vineyard. One day he made the mistake of getting as drunk as a skunk from the fruits of his labor. One of his sons named Ham went into his father's tent and saw Noah lying naked on the bed. Instead of keeping quiet about what he had seen out of respect for his father, Ham went outside and started talking about it with his brothers.

The other two brothers responded correctly to what Ham told them. They carried a blanket into the tent to cover their father's nakedness, walking backwards to the bed to respect his privacy.

So what did Ham do wrong? He exposed the nakedness of his God-ordained authority. Because of Ham's disrespect, God cursed him, while at the same time He blessed Ham's brothers.

You see, we live in a society that has such little respect for authority. That's why many Christians are not receiving answers to their prayers — because they don't understand the parameters of respect. They either don't realize or they refuse to comply with the principle that they are never to exploit, bear tales, or have an opinion of their assigned leaders' mistakes.

David: The Epitome of Respect

David was one man who understood this principle very well, and it was David's respect for his authority in his earlier years that helped him when he was older. Second Samuel 11 tells of the time a middle-aged King David fell into grave sin when he committed adultery with Bathsheba and then had her husband, Uriah the Hittite, murdered. No one at the time knew the reason David wasn't stoned to death for these sins because that was the punishment commanded by the Law. But I'm going to show you why David was spared from being stoned.

In First Samuel 24, we learn of the time many years earlier when King Saul came into a cave near Engedi to relieve himself. Unbeknownst to him, however, David and his men were hiding deeper in that same cave. Saul had long been on a jealous quest to kill David, so David's men said to their leader, "...This is the day of which the Lord said to you, 'Behold, I will deliver your enemy into your hand, that you may do to him as it seems good to you....'"

David listened to his men "...and secretly cut off a corner of Saul's robe" (v. 4). However, notice what it says next:

> Now it happened afterward that David's heart troubled him [one translation even says that David's heart *smote* him] because he had cut Saul's robe.
> And he said to his men, "The Lord forbid that I should do this thing to my master, the Lord's anointed, to stretch out my hand against him, seeing he is the anointed of the Lord."
>
> 1 Samuel 24:5,6

Then later something similar happened in the Wilderness of Ziph, where King Saul and his men were encamped one night while hunting David and his men.

So David arose and came to the place where Saul had encamped. And David saw the place where Saul lay, and Abner the son of Ner, the commander of his army. Now Saul lay within the camp, with the people encamped all around him....

Then Abishai said to David, "God has delivered your enemy into your hand this day. Now therefore, please, let me strike him at once with the spear, right to the earth; and I will not have to strike him a second time!"

And David said to Abishai, "Do not destroy him; for who can stretch out his hand against the Lord's anointed, and be guiltless?"

David said furthermore, "As the Lord lives, the Lord shall strike him, or his day shall come to die, or he shall go out to battle and perish.

"The Lord forbid that I should stretch out my hand against the Lord's anointed. But please, take now the spear and the jug of water that are by his head, and let us go."

1 Samuel 26:5,8-11

These passages of Scripture give us the reason David was never stoned to death for his sin later in life. *Twice David spared the anointed's life.* Twice he had opportunity to destroy the man who pursued him but refused to raise a finger against him. Twice David said, "Saul will be taken care of. God will deal with him in time. But as for me, I will not touch the Lord's anointed. I'm not going to touch the person God has called to that position."

David operated continually in respect toward his authorities and thus multiplied his life investment by adding many more years to his life!

Respect Your Future Harvest

When you follow David's example and live in respect toward your authorities on the job, you are actually respecting your God-ordained assignment. Ephesians 6:8 gives *you* a promise from God that is then yours to claim: **"...Whatever good anyone does, he will receive the same from the Lord, whether he is a slave or free."**

This goes along with the law of sowing and reaping as stated in Galatians 6:7,8:

Do not be deceived, God is not mocked; for whatever a man sows, that he will also reap.

For he who sows to his flesh will of the flesh reap corruption, but he who sows to the Spirit will of the Spirit reap everlasting life.

This, then, is the principle to remember:

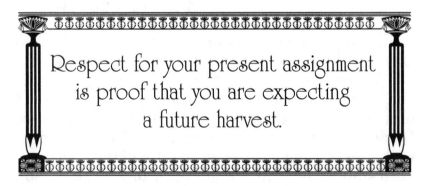

Respect for your present assignment
is proof that you are expecting
a future harvest.

If we don't care at all about our future, we can live disrespectfully, because disrespectful people always reap a negative harvest from the bad seeds they have sown.

That's why people who are disrespectful never get anywhere in life. That's also why it is crucial that we live respectfully before others in the workplace and in every other area of our lives if we truly care about multiplying our life investment and protecting our future.

Verse 9 goes on to say, **"And let us not grow weary while doing good, for in due season we shall reap if we do not lose heart."** It's very easy to become weary in this arena of respect because respect isn't a quality that our generation grew up with. In fact, it would be accurate to say that we have grown up in the age of disrespect. So God exhorts us, **"Let us not grow tired of doing good, for, unless we throw in our hand, the ultimate harvest is assured."**[1]

I have personally determined that I will not become weary in well-doing. I will not throw in my hand and stop showing respect to those God has assigned to be over me. Therefore, I know that the ultimate harvest of my life will surely come!

Some people don't believe that. They have the idea that they will somehow be on the losing end if they always show respect to people at their job. But

[1]J. B. Phillips, *The New Testament in Modern English* (New York: The MacMillan Co., 1962), p. 420.

103

the truth is, they will find themselves in a better situation than they could have ever thought possible if they will only live respectfully toward others!

For me, it's very simple. I do what I'm asked to do. I don't ask why I need to do it. I don't even think about it. I don't give people my opinions who are over me in the Lord. I just say, "Whatever you say, you're right. Just tell me what you'd like me to do. I may need clarification about what you're asking of me, but I'll never challenge you." By maintaining that respectful attitude, I am respecting my future harvest so I can become all I need to become for God.

So ask yourself these questions:

- *What am I doing with my life investment in the arena of respect?*

- *What quality of seed am I sowing into my relationships at my job?*

- *Are people at work better off or worse off because of how I treat them?*

I'm telling you, friend, the moment you embrace this vital principle and begin to truly respect those you work with and those who are over you in authority, it will begin to change your experience in the workplace. It will change the way your employer views you. It will change the way your fellow employees view you. And it will multiply your opportunities for promotion as you launch into the next level at your job!

Continually Strive To Excel

Let me give you another question that you should continually ask yourself in order to receive the greatest return on your life investment:

- *Am I continuing to excel toward my 100-percent potential?*

When you make this question your measuring stick for your performance in the workplace, people begin to say, "You know, you're a perfectionist." But whenever people tell me that, I just respond, "No, I'm not a perfectionist. I'm just an 'excellence-ist'!"

You see, perfection is God, but excellence is something attainable for us — a standard we can all begin to move toward. We can all become better every day in *every* area of our lives!

I want to excel in what God has called me to do. I want to be better at fulfilling that call tomorrow, next week, and next month than I am today. That's how I operate every day of my life. I can never be perfect this side of Heaven, but I *can* be excellent.

When you continually strive to excel, something is changing on the inside of you all the time. You may have taken the necessary steps to reach the next level. You may even be the biggest and the best fish in a little pond. But do you know what God does when you reach that point? He puts you in a bigger pond, where once again you're the smallest fish!

Why does God do that? Because He wants you to grow to be an even bigger fish!

You see, if you keep fish in a small aquarium, those fish will stay small. But when you put those same fish in a larger aquarium, you've given them the means to grow to their greatest potential.

That's what God does for you as well. He gives you room to excel within the level you are presently at. Then He promotes you so you can continue to grow in your divinely ordained gifts and callings.

Excellence is a continuing process, whereas perfection is the condition of having arrived at something. As long as you are striving to excel, you are moving in the direction of your future.

Are You a Finisher, Or Just a Starter?

Here's another question to ask yourself in order to evaluate whether or not you're moving forward on the road to multiplying your life investment:

- *Have I been faithful enough in my position at work to be approached by an expert in the field I'm in because he has recognized my desire for and my pursuit of excellence?*

In Second Timothy 2:15, the Bible describes this quality of diligent faithfulness:

Be diligent to present yourself approved to God, a worker who does not need to be ashamed, rightly dividing the word of truth.

We can't put the blame on someone else if we have never gotten the attention of our superiors at work. It isn't someone else's responsibility to make sure that happens; it's *ours*.

Get ahold of this fact:

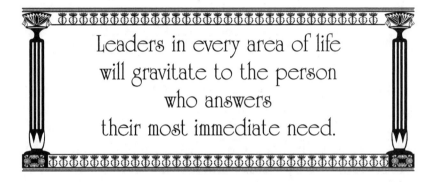

Leaders in every area of life will gravitate to the person who answers their most immediate need.

This principle includes business owners and supervisors in the workplace. It also explains one of the main reasons an employee's supervisor might go around him to get to someone else who actually has a lower position than he does.

This situation usually develops because, at one time or another, that employee was asked to do something and he didn't do it. So the supervisor concludes that he can't count on the employee and starts gravitating instead to the one who is the "go-to" person. That's the person who says every time, "I can do that, Sir. I'll take care of it." And the "go-to" person doesn't just say he'll do it — he actually *does* it.

In order to be the person *your* employer gravitates toward when he needs something, follow this principle:

107

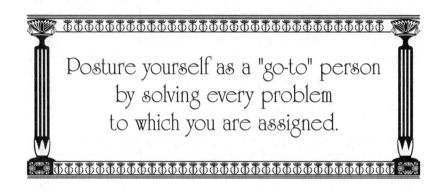

Posture yourself as a "go-to" person
by solving every problem
to which you are assigned.

You see, most people are awesome starters, but very few are good finishers. They start well, but they just can't bring their goal to completion. They can talk a good talk; they can sell themselves with their words. But, ultimately, they can't make what they have said happen.

In the workplace, these people may be given the benefit of the doubt for a few years. But eventually their superiors will start to go around them to find someone who will actually bring the assigned task to completion.

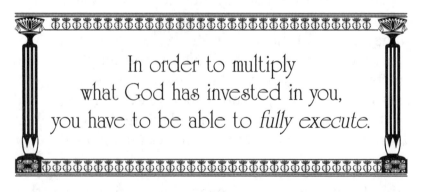

In order to multiply
what God has invested in you,
you have to be able to *fully execute.*

If I had to choose one thing that most frustrates me, it's the frustration I experience when people

108

don't fully execute to completion what they have said they would do. I've had international ministers tell me, "I'm going to take care of this. I'm going to help your ministry in this way." So I spend time getting myself into position for their words to come to pass — and then nothing happens. It was all a waste of time.

By contrast, I have a particular minister friend in my life who is not only a good starter but a great finisher. He calls me and says things like, "I have scheduled you to speak at this conference, Robb. This person will be in contact with you concerning that engagement, and I'll talk to you next week to make sure everything has been taken care of." Now, *that's* an executor!

If *you* want to be known as a faithful executor as well, make this your guiding principle:

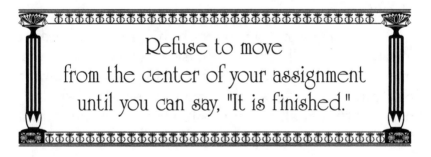

Refuse to move
from the center of your assignment
until you can say, "It is finished."

That's the way you build a reputation as a finisher. You cannot fail if you will not quit!

Never Stop Moving Forward

You are a living being. You cannot be stationary in life. You are either going forward or backwards at any given moment. You are either multiplying your life investment, or you are squandering it through neglect and disuse. You are either taking steps toward God's best, or you are moving backwards toward mediocrity.

The first thing that happens when you go backwards is that you begin to go without. Then you start to think, *I knew this faith walk would never work,* and your wrong thoughts take you another step backwards. If you keep going that direction, your life will end up worse off than it was when you first began your walk with God. Why? Because you didn't keep your focus on God and the multiplication of His gifts and talents in your life.

So where do you want to go in life? What is it that you want to achieve in the days and years to come? What are you currently doing toward the fulfillment of your goals?

I want to encourage you with this thought: Because of what Jesus Christ has done for you, you can press in. You can multiply your life investment beyond anything you've ever imagined. There is absolutely nothing that shall be impossible to you as you pursue excellence in what God has called you to do.

Just leave behind once and for all any words you've heard over the years that have hindered you, such as, "You'll never make it. You're no good. Things aren't going to work out for you." Never forget what Ephesians 6:8 (*KJV*) says: **"...Whatsoever good thing any man doeth, the same shall he receive of the Lord...."**

God didn't say you're going to receive those good things from another man. He said you are going to receive from *Him* — and that includes supernatural favor and promotion in the workplace!

PRINCIPLES FOR MULTIPLYING YOUR LIFE INVESTMENT

★ **All of us have twenty-four hours each day. How we spend our twenty-four hours will determine the outcome of our lives.**

★ **The only way to multiply your life investments and accelerate your growth is by pursuing excellence in the arenas of your intended focus.**

★ **Whatever you respect moves toward you, and whatever you disrespect distances itself from you.**

★ **A Person of Excellence assesses who and what he is in every relationship and then postures himself accordingly.**

★ **A Person of Excellence never corrects upwards.**

★ **Know the people from whom God intends for you to access information, because these are the people who help determine the outcome of your life.**

★ **Taking your employer for granted will ruin the harvest you are designed to receive from the field in which God has set you.**

111

★ Never allow the invitation to intimacy to be destroyed by the contempt of familiarity.

★ Never hold an opinion about people God has called to lead you in your life.

★ We must never allow ourselves the luxury of questioning anything about those in authority over us.

★ God has given you a position that takes 100 percent of your focus. The moment you start criticizing your employer is the moment you have moved off the post to which you have been assigned.

★ We must always remember that God has called us to cover and never to expose our authority's nakedness.

★ Respect for your present assignment is proof that you are expecting a future harvest.

★ Leaders in every area of life will gravitate to the person who answers their most immediate need.

★ Posture yourself as a "go-to" person by solving every problem to which you are assigned.

★ In order to multiply what God has invested in you, you have to be able to *fully execute.*

★ Refuse to move from the center of your assignment until you can say, "It is finished."

NOTES:

NOTES:

MAKE YOUR DREAM OF PROMOTION A REALITY

Let's say you have set some important goals for yourself at your job, and you have a good idea of what you want to achieve there. One of the dreams in your heart is to be promoted to a higher position with greater responsibility. Well, this is my question to you:

Are you going to make your dream of promotion come to pass, or is that dream going to remain mere theory — a nice thought, but something never to be realized?

Personally, I love to dream. I love to take a look into the future at all that God is going to cause me to become and what He is going to accomplish through me. But I realize that I can't just dream. I have to learn how to make my God-given dreams come to pass. It won't do me a bit of good if I can't take my dream and transfer it into the natural realm so I can walk it out day by day.

You might say, "Well, I'm not a dreamer or an idealist; I'm a pragmatist." But being a pragmatist can actually be a negative quality if it means you're so practical that you never have any desires. God designed you to dream *big* regarding His plan for your life. He wants you to reach your goals of success and promotion as you continually strive to become better at what you do.

It's amazing how many Christians have short attention spans, never sticking with their dreams long enough to see them come to pass. They may jump and shout and get all excited when someone teaches on scriptural success principles, but they don't know how to make those principles work for themselves.

Success principles will only frustrate a person who will not apply them to his life. They will condemn anyone who will not act on them, because that person knows what he should do and yet doesn't do it. James 4:17 (*NAS*) explains how God sees this type of person:

...To one who knows the right thing to do, and does not do it, to him it is sin.

The truth is, if we are hearing the Word but not doing the Word, we are living in a pipe dream. We may dream of success and promotion in our career or at our place of employment, but we will never see that dream come to pass until we put God's principles into practice in our lives.

What does that mean? Precisely this:

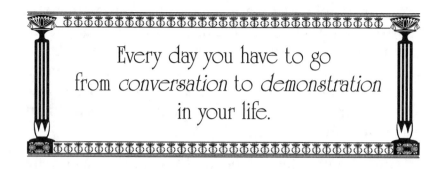

Every day you have to go from *conversation* to *demonstration* in your life.

This principle certainly includes the workplace, because you can't separate any part of your life from your walk with God. Everything you do at your job is a reflection of whether or not you are a doer and not just a hearer of the Word.

That's why Jesus said in Matthew 15:8 (*KJV*):

This people draweth nigh unto me with their mouth, and honoureth me with their lips; but their heart is far from me.

He was saying, "I hear all the good words, but that doesn't really mean anything if you don't back up those words with your actions. You'll never see My promises fulfilled in your life if your conversation doesn't become demonstration."

Freedom From the Greatest Enemy of Dreams: *Fear*

Once I took some time to ponder this question: *If I had to pick one thing that most often keeps a person who knows the answers from bringing his dreams to pass in his life, what would that one thing be?*

After thinking about it awhile, I realized the answer was obvious: The thing that hinders people the most from fulfilling their dreams is *fear*. Luke 21:26 says men's hearts fail them for fear of things to come. Then in Proverbs 29:25, it says, **"The fear of man brings a snare, but whoever trusts in the Lord shall be safe."**

But David offers hope in this matter when he says in Psalm 118:6:

The Lord is on my side; I will not fear. What can man do to me?

When someone speaks this way, you automatically know obstacles are being presented to him that could ultimately destroy him if he allowed them to. Nevertheless, David proclaimed, "I'm not going to fear! After all, what can man do to me?"

How could David say that? How could he have such great confidence in the knowledge that God would take care of him?

God has provided a place for the believer where he can live above all the pulls, all the controls, and all the guilt trips of this life, a place where he is continually shielded by God's grace from every attack of fear and intimidation. Moses wrote of this holy place in Psalm 91:

He that dwelleth in the secret place of the most High shall abide under the shadow of the Almighty.

I will say of the Lord, He is my refuge and my fortress: my God; in him will I trust.

Surely he shall deliver thee from the snare of the fowler, and from the noisome pestilence.

He shall cover thee with his feathers, and under his wings shalt thou trust: his truth shall be thy shield and buckler.

Psalm 91:1-4 *KJV*

In verse 2, Moses speaks of himself, saying in essence, "I'm going to say this about the Lord as it concerns me: *He is my refuge and my fortress.*"

But in the other three verses, Moses is preaching to *you*. He tells you, "If you will dwell in the secret place of the Most High, you will abide under the shadow of the Almighty. That's the place where you will be protected from all fear and every attack of the enemy. God will cover you with his feathers, and under His wings will you trust. His truth will be your shield and your buckler."

Moses is preaching to you about God's covenant of protection so you can grab ahold of that covenant by faith and dwell in the secret place of the Most High on a daily basis. It is in this place where God's Presence resides that a person can actually refuse to be conformed to this world's way of doing things.

Moses writes further about what it is like to dwell in that secret place, safe from every attack of fear:

119

A thousand shall fall at thy side, and ten thousand at thy right hand; but it shall not come nigh thee....

There shall no evil befall thee, neither shall any plague come nigh thy dwelling.

For he shall give his angels charge over thee, to keep thee in all thy ways.

They shall bear thee up in their hands, lest thou dash thy foot against a stone....

With long life will I satisfy him [the one who sets his love on Me]**, and shew him my salvation.**

Psalm 91:7,10-12,16 *KJV*

In this secret place of the Most High, God satisfies His people with long and abundant life. But how it is possible to go through each day in the workplace without conforming to the ideas of this world? Romans 12:2 tells us:

And do not be conformed to this world [don't allow your outward appearance and your outward actions to be driven and molded by this world]**, but be transformed by the renewing of your mind, that you may prove what is that good and acceptable and perfect will of God.**

As you are transformed by the Word of God, your life in the workplace will begin to demonstrate the good, the acceptable, and the perfect will of God. The fear that has hindered your dream of promotion in the past — whether fear of failure, fear of what other people will think, or fear of the future — will become a thing of the past as you learn to say along with David, "The Lord is on my side; I will not fear. What can man do to me?"

The Most Important Truth To Learn

Without the transformation process that comes through renewing our minds with God's Word, the circumstances and pressures of life will mold and press us into becoming something God never wanted us to be. We will be easily taken in by the world's mindsets, attitudes, and prejudices, which will then taint every situation we face at our jobs, in our homes, and in every other area of life.

But you and I have been called by God to live above the worldly mindsets and prejudices of this life. In Galatians 3:26-29, the apostle Paul reminded the Galatian church of this very fact:

For you are all sons of God through faith in Christ Jesus.

For as many of you as were baptized into Christ have put on Christ.

There is neither Jew nor Greek, there is neither slave nor free, there is neither male nor female; for you are all one in Christ Jesus.

And if you are Christ's, then you are Abraham's seed, and heirs according to the promise.

Paul was telling the Galatian church this important truth:

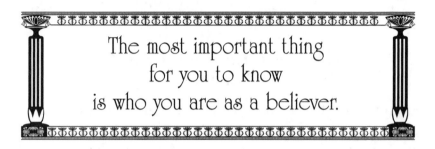

The most important thing
for you to know
is who you are as a believer.

Nothing else was more important for the Galatians to understand than what Christ had made them through His death and resurrection.

You see, the Galatians were attempting once again to be conformed to the ways of Judaism and to what the world wanted to impose upon them. So the apostle Paul wrote to them, saying in essence, "Look, Galatians, God has provided a secret place for us where we can live above the influences and pressures the world wants to place on us. There is a place where you and I as believers can dwell continually, no longer controlled, molded, or manipulated with the leaven of this earth — a place where we can live life in harmony with God and as overcomers in this world."

God Determines Your Position in Life

When you dwell in the secret place of the Most High, every dream that God has placed in your heart becomes a reality waiting to happen. You begin to understand a key principle:

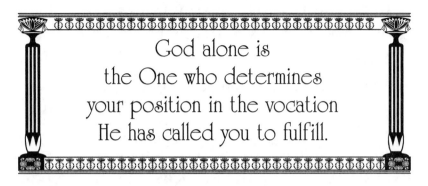

God alone is
the One who determines
your position in the vocation
He has called you to fulfill.

This is what I love about John the Baptist. He understood this principle and absolutely refused to violate it during his short lifetime.

Jesus Himself said that John the Baptist was the greatest prophet ever born of a woman (Luke 7:28). Multitudes of people would go out into the desert on a daily basis to hear John preach his blunt message: "Repent, for the Kingdom of Heaven is at hand!"

One day the priests and Levites asked him, "Listen, John, tell us who you are. Are you Elijah?" But John simply answered, "No." (*See* John 1:19-23.)

Now, think for a moment about how John the Baptist could have responded. After all, he was operating an extremely successful ministry! When these Jewish leaders asked him, "Are you Elijah?" he could have said, "Well, I'm a prophet like Elijah."

Or when they asked, "Are you the Prophet?" he could have responded, "Just look around at all the people coming to hear me preach. Can't you see what's happening here? Isn't it obvious that I'm a great prophet?"

But John didn't say that. When the priests and Levites asked, "Are you the Prophet?" he just said, "No, I'm not."

"Well, we've been sent out here to find out who you are. So what do you have to say about yourself?"

Look at John's humble response: **"...I am the voice of one crying in the wilderness, Make straight the way of the Lord, as said the prophet Esaias"** (v. 23 *KJV*).

Now, remember, this was the greatest prophet of all time and the cousin of the Messiah. But John didn't say, "Hey, that's my cousin! See, we even look alike. My mom is His mom's aunt. I'm bigger and tougher than He is, because I'm six months older!"

No, John never took advantage of his relationship to Jesus. We can't even tell from the Scriptures whether or not John ever directly addressed Jesus! But we do know this: When John, the greatest prophet ever born of a woman, sat at the side of the road and watched Jesus walk by, he did nothing but draw people's attention toward Jesus: **"...Behold! The Lamb of God who takes away the sin of the world!"** (John 1:29).

Later, John's disciples came to their leader and said, "Listen, John, we need to do something new in our ministry. Jesus is stealing the limelight!" (John 3:26).

But John replied, "No, He must *increase,* and I must *decrease*" (v. 30).

Identify With That Which Is Written

John understood that his position in life was not determined by anyone but God. In the same way, you must live above the world's clamoring for the spotlight and the top positions. The position that God gives you in your vocation is better than any position the world could ever give you.

In the past, the world may have dealt you a death blow. You may have been told that you weren't going to make it in your career or business and that you were doomed to fail. But focus only on what *God* tells you. He says that greater is He who is in you than he that is in the world (John 4:4). He says that you are born of Him and therefore can overcome the world by your faith (1 John 5:4).

God has never said to you, "Well, you know, you were born on the wrong side of the tracks, so you're not going to make it. You were never meant to make it." If those lies have been bombarding your mind, you need to realize where they're coming from. Certainly they aren't coming from God!

God made us all winners; He didn't leave out even one of us. Remember what He said in Galatians 3:26,28:

For you are ALL sons of God through faith in Christ Jesus....
There is neither Jew nor Greek, there is neither slave nor free, there is neither male nor female; for you are ALL one in Christ Jesus.

Please believe me when I tell you this, friend: In redemption, it doesn't matter what your background is. It doesn't matter what nationality or race you are. You have been called by God to live above the world's ideas and prejudices. If you are a child of God, He has provided a place for you to dwell far above the things of the world, hidden in the secret place of His Presence where fear cannot come and where every God-given dream of success and promotion can be realized.

As a child of God through faith in the Lord Jesus Christ, you are an heir according to the promise. So don't ever let anyone tell you that you weren't meant to win!

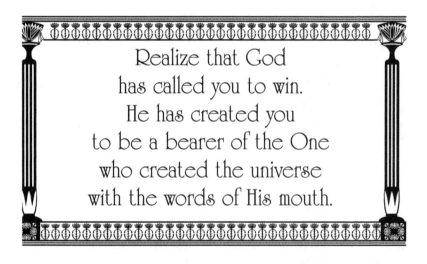

Realize that God has called you to win. He has created you to be a bearer of the One who created the universe with the words of His mouth.

That's why it doesn't matter what anyone at the job says or thinks about you. It doesn't matter if people say you are at a disadvantage because you don't have the necessary background or education or training or experience. You may have been surrounded your entire life by people who failed to realize their vocational dreams, but that doesn't mean *you* have to fail.

I made the decision long ago that it doesn't matter how I was raised. It doesn't matter who you think I am. I'm serving you notice right now — you are going to see me win! You may not be able to see the full manifestation of my victory right now, but just hide in the bushes and watch — because I'm going to win!

Don't think for one minute that I'm going to breathe and not win. It takes just as much effort to breathe and lose as it does to breathe and win, and I'm not a loser!

You have to develop the same confident trust in God's ability to promote you. It doesn't matter what your employer thinks or says about it. All that matters is what *God* has said and what you believe about yourself. God says that promotion comes from Him. He also says that as you think in your heart, so are you.

So what do you think about yourself? Perhaps you focus on the way you look on the outside, thinking, *You know, you're so unworthy. You can't make it. You're too stupid. You just can't get on top of things, can you? It works for everyone else, but it has never worked for you.* I guarantee you, those kind of thoughts aren't going to help you realize your dream of promotion!

127

Over the years as I have observed people who have succeeded in life, I have seen a common thread that runs through every one of them: *They all have a positive self-image.* Now, a positive self-image isn't bound to race or creed. It isn't contingent on what kind of background a person has or what side of the tracks he was born on. A positive attitude about oneself originates in a person's ability to identify with who he is in Jesus Christ.

So don't pick up your identity from your family or your background. Pick it up from that which is written. God told you that you could win, so it's up to you to believe that you are a winner! Don't allow one thought to stay in your mind that you're not going to achieve your dreams. You've been created to reach your full potential in Christ, but it will only happen as you place your identity in that which God has said about you.

Faithfulness:
The Foundation of Excellence

So what qualities must you demonstrate in the workplace to help you excel and eventually realize your dream of promotion?

For now, let's discuss one of the most important qualities you must possess in order to build a solid foundation of excellence in your life. That quality is *faithfulness.*

Proverbs 20:6 says this: **"Most men will proclaim each his own goodness, but who can find a faithful**

man?" That's a very good question that most employers are constantly asking themselves!

Many times people complain, "My supervisor doesn't like me, and I know that's the reason I'm not receiving a promotion."

Let me tell you something about superiors at work. *They don't really care about your personality; they care about your work and your productivity.*

I know some people who are very talented. I'm telling you, these people can hit a home run every time! The problem is, it's hard to find them to put them up to the plate to bat!

A person like that will say, "I'll be there at three o'clock." So you wait for him as the clock ticks away: four o'clock, five o'clock, six o'clock. Finally, he shows up and gives his excuse: "Oh, I'm sorry, I got caught up in something else. I tell you what — let's just do it tomorrow."

"All right, no problem," you say. "We'll go ahead and do it tomorrow."

The next day, it starts all over again. As you wait one, two, even three hours for this person to show up, you start thinking, *You know, I really love this guy's work, but he never does what he says he will do!*

Let me tell you something — the Bible never once says that leaders are to commit anything to spiritual "hot shots" whom they can't count on. Instead, Paul instructs Timothy:

And the things that you have heard from me among many witnesses, COMMIT THESE TO FAITHFUL MEN who will be able to teach others also.

2 Timothy 2:2

How does this apply to the workplace? Authority figures are looking to commit positions of responsibility to *faithful* people, not to unreliable "flashes in the pan." That's why Proverbs 28:20 says, **"A faithful man will abound with blessings, but he who hastens to be rich will not go unpunished."** A faithful man will reap many blessings, but the person who goes after the money will ultimately be destroyed.

Now, I know that doesn't seem to make sense to your natural mind. You may wonder, *But don't we all go to work so we can make a paycheck?*

So many people in today's world have learned how to live for their time *off* instead of for their time *on* the job. They spend much more time thinking about their vacation than what they can produce at their place of employment.

But you can't do that if you want to be known as a faithful person in the workplace. You have to live by this basic principle:

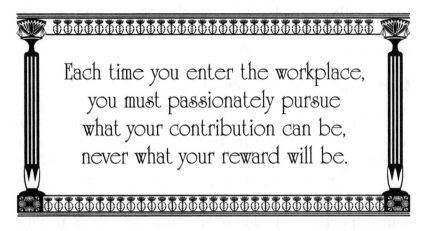

Each time you enter the workplace, you must passionately pursue what your contribution can be, never what your reward will be.

Characteristics of a Potential Leader

How do you become the foreman of the crew, the supervisor of the department, or the manager of the store? What else can you do besides develop faithfulness in your life that will make your employer take notice of you when promotion time comes around?

1. TAKE CARE OF YOUR PERSONAL APPEARANCE.

The man who owns the largest temporary employment agency in America today once said that more than 98 percent of people are hired for their jobs because of personal appearance. So ask yourself this:

- *How do I look when I go to work in the morning?*

- *What can I do to take a step up to another level in my personal appearance?*

Someone might say, "Well, yes, but my quality of work is good even if my appearance isn't." Well, that

131

isn't really true. If that person doesn't take care of the way he looks, he isn't going to take care of the way his work may look.

2. BECOME AN EXPERT ABOUT YOUR JOB.

Proverbs 1:5 (*NAS*) says, **"A wise man will hear and increase in learning...."** So become an expert in the field in which you work. Know things about your job that other people don't. Soon your supervisor won't ask anyone else questions about your expertise because every time he comes to you, you have the answers!

3. GIVE ATTENTION TO DETAIL.

If you want to receive a promotion and make more money, let me assure you — your employer doesn't have a problem with rewarding you for your performance. He has a problem rewarding you for a *poor* performance. Money isn't the issue. The real issue is whether or not you are detail-oriented.

I'll give you an example of what you might do if you are detail-oriented. Suppose you walked down an aisle at work and saw a piece of paper lying on the floor. As a detail-oriented employee, you would pick it up off the floor. You would *not* leave it there and think, *That's job security for the maintenance man!*

You may think I'm kidding, but this really is important to those in authority at the workplace. I've had many business owners say to me, "You know, that's right. I do look for employees who don't neglect the little details."

Many employees are just the opposite of being detail-oriented. For instance, when people are hired for a new job, they want to know, "How much will I make? How much vacation time will I get? How many sick days and holidays? How is the insurance package?" But then before they even start, too often they say things like, "By the way, I'll be late coming in tomorrow; I know that won't bother you." But employers are interested in employees who are punctual. Why? Because taking care of that one detail says a lot about a person's worth as an employee.

Recently I was sitting at a restaurant I often frequent, talking to the owner. As we talked, the owner pointed over to one particular table and asked, "Do you see the table setting over there on that table?" The elegant table setting he was referring to had a nicely folded cloth napkin, a knife, and a fork; however, the table setting was missing a spoon. Now, to a worker, that one little omission may mean nothing; but to an employer, it means everything.

Every employee who went to the bathroom had to walk by this particular table. During the hour I was there, each employee working that shift walked by the table, but no one ever put a spoon in the incomplete table setting. It wasn't as if everyone was too busy to take the time to do it. It was just that no one considered such a small problem important enough to fix.

The owner and I sat and watched as every person walked by without taking care of that small detail. Finally, he said, "You know, that's a good example of why I think everything a person does needs to be done in excellence."

Now, you may say, "Wow, Robb, you are really picky!"

You're right; I *am* picky. I don't like anything under my authority to be out of order. If I'm going to pay you, you are going to complete your task. And if I'm going to promote you, you must be detail-oriented!

So if you desire your employer to be impressed with you, give immediate and accurate attention to the matters he speaks to you about. As he talks to you, walk around with a little tape recorder or a clipboard to record his thoughts. Then immediately start following up on his instructions, and get back to him as soon as you can.

Immediate attention to detail will get you the recognition you long for. On the other hand, neglecting details will get you the kind of attention you hate. For instance, when you put off an assignment that your employer gives you, you're sending him the message, "Other things are more important to me than your instructions." This may disqualify you from the future you desire with your place of employment.

Do you know what happens when you put off an assigned task? You end up procrastinating even more. Then whenever you remember that responsibility you've been putting off, you cringe and think, *Oh, man, it's been awhile since the boss asked me to do that. Now I don't want to do it because as soon as I do, he will remember his instructions to me and realize that I'm late in getting it done.* So the procrastination goes on a few more days. Soon you're praying that your employer will forget the matter altogether!

But never fear — your employer may be delayed in getting back to you, but he didn't forget. So if you want to receive positive attention from him, your only recourse is to develop this quality of immediate attention to detail in your life.

This is an especially important principle to understand given the current economic situation in the world today. Many companies all over the world have downsized in one way or another. It's very possible that people have gotten laid off from the company where you work.

As companies get smaller, more and more people will be losing their jobs. How do you make sure that you're not one of them? *By giving attention to detail.* Why? Because an employer wants to surround himself with people who will do what he asks them to do as soon as he asks them to do it.

Remember, your employer doesn't live his life in his "hard drive," or his long-term memory; he lives almost solely in his "ram" — his immediate memory.

What is most important to him is that which is in his mind right now.

Suppose your superior at work says to you, "But I asked you for that last week."

"Um, yeah, but I didn't have a chance to get to it."

"Well, do you think you could get to it today?"

"Yeah, I'll try."

The "I'll try" response may work once, but it won't keep working for you because you're showing your superior that you don't care. If you keep putting things off, he will eventually find someone else to meet that need in the workplace.

Promotion only comes when you are detail-oriented. That's why this principle holds true:

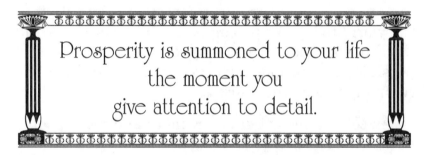

Prosperity is summoned to your life
the moment you
give attention to detail.

4. DO MORE THAN IS EXPECTED OF YOU.

If you want your employer's attention, you have to:

- *do what he asks you to do;*
- *do it fast; and*
- *do it right.*

Immediately you become the person your employer is looking for because you're the one who does what he asks quickly and without complaint.

However, you must remember this:

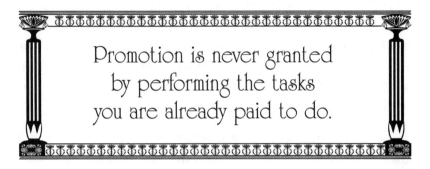

Promotion is never granted by performing the tasks you are already paid to do.

That's why you must do *more* than what is expected of you.

In Matthew 5:41, Jesus said it like this: **"And whoever compels you to go one mile, go with him two."** Be willing to go the extra mile for your supervisor.

"Yes, but I'm so busy," you may say.

I understand, but you have to realize that everyone is busy, not just you. If you are overloaded when a task is asked of you, go to your supervisor and ask him to prioritize your assigned tasks for you.

"Which would you like me to complete first, Sir? Would you like what you just asked me for? Or would you like me to finish the project you gave me yesterday?"

Ask your supervisor to do the prioritizing; don't do it yourself. No matter what you choose — even if it is the right decision — it stands a good chance of being misconstrued as the wrong choice to make.

So tell your supervisor, "This is what I have on my schedule, and you'd like me to fit in this new assignment. I need this much time to complete the new assignment. So where would you like me to put it in my schedule of tasks I need to complete for you?"

Responding to your superiors without arguments makes your life so much easier. Saying, "Yes, Sir, whatever you'd like" gets you so much further than does the thought, *How dare you give me more work!* or the look that shows the displeasure you are presently feeling. All you've done by getting upset like that is impair your future because, without more work, you don't have a job!

You see, there are two different ways to make people dependent on you. One is to lie to them in order to make them believe you're necessary. The other is to make yourself so valuable that they can't live without you!

5. BE HONEST ABOUT MISTAKES.

If you've made a mistake, go to your superior and let him know what happened. Proverbs 28:13 says, **"He who covers his sins will not prosper, but whoever confesses and forsakes them will have mercy."**

Don't ever blame-shift or put the responsibility for your mistakes on someone else.

You may ask, "But what if another person had something to do with the problem?"

But that isn't the reason you're talking to your superior about the matter. You're not there to tell on some other person; you're there to tell on *yourself*. You're there to say, "Sir, I made a mistake"; then your supervisor can tell you what to do to correct the problem.

Choose To Be an Asset To Your Employer

Besides the characteristics of potential leadership that we just talked about, remember this: *Every day you go to work, you are there to be a problem-solver in any way you can.*

That's what I endeavored to do years ago while working at a parcel delivery service. When I first came to this company to apply for a job, I had just been released from the mental institution where I had come to Christ. I had no job, no money, no experience — I seemed to have nothing of value to offer the company. But I went over anyway and filled out an application.

My heart sank as I looked at all the questions on the application. The first one was "Have you ever been on drugs?" (I checked the "Yes" box.) "Have you ever had a bad back?" (Another "Yes.") "When was the last time your back hurt you?" (I wrote "Recently.") "Have you ever had mental problems?"

139

(Here we go again: "Yes.") "Have you ever been institutionalized?" ("Yes" again!)

The interviewer just watched me as I checked all those "wrong" answers. But, amazingly, when I had completed the application, he said, "Okay, you're hired!"

"But," he added, "you need to shave off your beard."

Now, when I heard that, I didn't start a class-action suit. I didn't say, "Well, I'm going to get a bunch of people together to protest because we want to keep our beards!" No, I just asked the man, "Do you have a razor? I'll do it right now." You see, from the very beginning, I was determined to become a problem-solver for my superiors at my new job.

However, I had been hired as Christmas help. That meant when December 24 came, it was time to say good-bye!

It was hard to go when the company laid me off on Christmas Eve. I loved my job there. I thought it was the greatest company to work for in the world and enjoyed every moment of it because, when I went out delivering packages, I was working as unto the Lord.

When the company laid me off, my supervisor said, "Maybe you'll have the chance to work here again in a few months. We'll call you if we have an opening." But I didn't wait for them to call me; I called *them* twice a week.

I'd say, "I just want to let you know one thing. I came here to work for your company because I'm good for you. I'm here to make you money. I want to help bring your company further along than you've ever been before. And I just want to let you know that you will never have one second of a problem with this man. I want to be part of your answer, not part of your problem."

Well, they hired me again, and I made good on my promise. I'd go to my supervisor every morning and say, "Boss, I want to tell you exactly why I'm here today. I am not here to earn money. I am here for the express purpose of getting you a promotion."

I didn't care if I received a promotion. I wasn't trying to be a good employee just so I could get ahead. I was working for my supervisor's promotion because of my love for God.

You see, God doesn't want your motivation for doing well at your job to be the fear of not having a job. That isn't how He created you. He created you to succeed because *He* is successful. He created you to multiply because *He* is a multiplier. He created you to walk in love toward your employer because His very nature is love.

So if you ever want to fulfill your own dream of promotion, follow this principle that I have followed since I first became a believer:

141

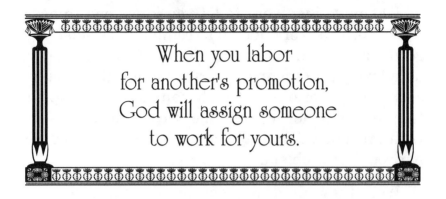

When you labor
for another's promotion,
God will assign someone
to work for yours.

The apostle Paul takes this subject even further in Ephesians 6. In dealing with employer-employee relationships, he told the Ephesian believers that they were to work as unto God even when they didn't get paid for their work.

Servants (slaves), be obedient to those who are your physical masters, having respect for them and eager concern to please them, in singleness of motive and with all your heart, as [service] to Christ [Himself].

Ephesians 6:5 *AMP*

Your sincerity of heart isn't directed toward your employer. You are to excel in your work because of your sincere heart unto the Lord Jesus Christ.

You see, your superior at work may make fun of you when you endeavor to live according to these principles of excellence. He may think, *Man, this person can't be real. No one is like this!* Then he may try to give you a huge amount of work to see if he can break you and make you negative.

I recall one day when I had so much work, I got a little nervous. That was the day my supervisor told me, "I'm going to bury you with work."

I answered, "Excuse me, Sir, but do you realize you don't have enough work or enough trucks to bury me? And do you know what else? You *can't* destroy me."

You see, I knew about that place of protection where you and I live in God. I knew I was living in the secret place of the Most High, dwelling under the shadow of His wings.

Have you ever seen children stand in front of a high fence with a big, mean dog on the other side of it? That dog backs up to get a good run at them, but all he receives for his trouble is a headache and a bite of the fence! Meanwhile, the children stand there laughing at the dog's helplessness to hurt them.

That's exactly how it is in the workplace when you have an employer who wants to destroy you. No man can keep you from being promoted just because you don't live by his lower standards. When you live by a higher standard than your employer does, there is nothing he can say, even though it may frustrate him that he can't control you.

You see, the way you give someone else control over you is by letting him know he has something you want. So just maintain the attitude, "No man can give me anything; my promotion comes from the Lord!" John the Baptist said it like this: **"...A man can receive nothing unless it has been given to him from heaven"** (John 3:27).

Let me reiterate what you can do for a supervisor who doesn't seem to like you or is treating you unfairly:

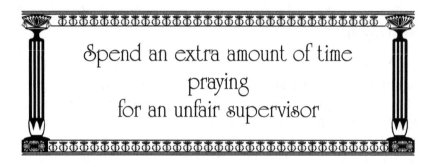

Spend an extra amount of time praying for an unfair supervisor

Allow God to promote your superior right out of your life! Say, "God, I'm asking you to bless my supervisor. He stands in the way of Your will, Lord, so I ask You to save him or move him up. Meanwhile, I'm going to do my work as unto You, Father."

(Notice, you are to pray that God would move your supervisor *up*, not *down*. Bitterness wants a person to be moved to a lower level; the love of God wants him to be blessed as he moves *up*.)

Let God's Will Be Your Focus, Not Making More Money

Every one of us desires to prosper at our jobs. That's why God gives us scriptural principles to guide us along the way to that goal. For example,

144

Colossians 3 has two important verses that serve as basic guiding principles to follow as we pursue our dreams, including our dream of promotion in the workplace:

And whatever you do in word or deed, do all in the name of the Lord Jesus, giving thanks to God the Father through Him....

And whatever you do, do it heartily, as to the Lord and not to men.

Colossians 3:17,23

Here's one thing we can conclude from these verses: Although the desire to prosper at our jobs is a good desire, that doesn't mean that our driving motive for working at a job should be to make money.

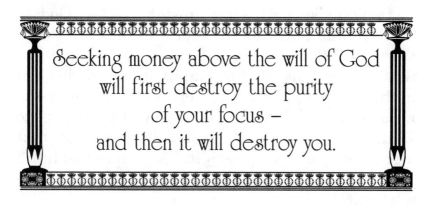

Seeking money above the will of God will first destroy the purity of your focus – and then it will destroy you.

You may say, "Wait a second! I'm out there working real hard. I deserve to make good money!"

Well, have you found out what God's will is for your life yet? Is it His will that you be a paymaster in the Kingdom of God? Does God want you to go out there in the business world and become tremendously successful so you can hire a number of people and bless multitudes through your generous giving into God's Kingdom? Do you know for sure that this is God's will for you?

If that is God's will for your life, friend, you have to move in that direction. But that doesn't mean you are to move in the direction of *money*. Absolutely everything you do is to be done *as unto the Lord and for His glory.*

The problem with too many of us is that we go after the benefit of our actions instead of making our focus the fulfillment of God's will *through* our actions. Then after using God's principles to prosper outside of His will, some of us begin to backslide.

Don't make that same mistake. Allow God to bring you up to the level He desires to bring you at your job. When you do it God's way — when you refuse to be controlled or manipulated, but instead faithfully serve with a sincere heart as unto the Lord — you *will* be rewarded. You will not only go to a higher level at work, you will *remain* at that higher level once you reach it. *That's* how you fulfill your dream of promotion and success in the workplace!

PRINCIPLES FOR MAKING YOUR DREAM OF PROMOTION A REALITY

★ Every day you have to go from *conversation* to *demonstration* in your life.

★ The most important thing for you to know is who you are as a believer.

★ God alone is the One who determines your position in the vocation He has called you to fulfill.

★ Realize that God has called you to win. He has created you to be a bearer of the One who created the universe with the words of His mouth.

★ Each time you enter the workplace, you must passionately pursue what your contribution can be, never what your reward will be.

★ Prosperity is summoned to your life the moment you give attention to detail.

★ Promotion is never granted by performing the tasks you are already paid to do.

★ When you labor for another's promotion, God will assign someone to work for yours.

★ Spend an extra amount of time praying for an unfair supervisor to get a promotion.

★ Seeking money above the will of God will first destroy the purity of your focus — and then it will destroy you.

NOTES:

CHAPTER FOUR

KEY TO SUCCESS: BECOME A PROBLEM-SOLVER

Did you know God is a poor loser? Every time we fail, He cries. After all, He has invested a lot in us — His Spirit, His wisdom, the very blood of His Son. That's why He has made it possible for us to always triumph in Christ. He never calls us to lose, no matter what situation we may face.

Now thanks be to God who always leads us in triumph in Christ, and through us diffuses the fragrance of His knowledge in every place.

2 Corinthians 2:14

Yet despite all God has done for His children, many believers are losers going somewhere to happen. I've always been very interested in knowing why this is the case.

Given our high rate of failure as believers in the past, I wanted to find out how God makes good things happen for us. How do doors of opportunity and promotion open for us in life so we can use our God-given gifts to the full extent that God intended?

Everything God Has Created Solves a Problem

One of the greatest keys I've found for opening doors that lead to God's perfect will is this:

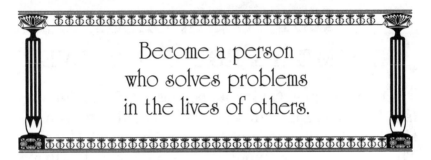

Become a person
who solves problems
in the lives of others.

You see, every problem in life has a solution. Everything God has created, He has created to solve a problem.

- Doctors solve health problems.
- Dentists solve teeth problems.
- Lawyers solve legal problems.
- Ministers solve spiritual problems.
- Your eyeglasses solve your reading problems.
- Your clothes solve a nakedness problem.

We can trace this truth all the way back to the beginning. God had a problem; He wanted a family. So God created Adam to solve His problem.

Then Adam had a problem. "How can that be?" you may ask. "How could Adam have a problem when he had God's complete and undivided attention?" Because even though a person has God in his life, he will still have problems that need to be solved.

God identified Adam's problem in Genesis 2:18 when He said, **"...It is not good that man should be alone...."** God was saying, "I see a problem that Adam has, and I am going to solve it." Thus, woman was created to solve man's problem of loneliness.

People often don't understand this, but even Satan solves a problem for God. Think about it — after Satan's rebellion in Heaven, why didn't God just get rid of Satan right then and there?

God wanted a family, and He wanted that family to choose to fellowship with Him. But without a true choice, God could not be chosen. Then Satan came in to distract Adam and Eve away from God. In that distraction, man had to use the free will God had given him. Which kingdom would he choose: God's Kingdom or Satan's kingdom of darkness?

This is why the negative side of life can actually be seen to solve a problem. *You can actually choose on purpose to pursue a successful outcome for your life.*

If you look at Isaiah 61:1-3, you'll find that God sent Jesus to solve every problem man could ever have.

- He preaches good news of prosperity to the poor.

- He heals the broken-hearted.

- He proclaims liberty to the captives.

- He opens the prison doors to those who are bound.

- He comforts all who mourn.

- He trades beauty for ashes, the oil of joy for mourning, and the garment of praise for the spirit of heaviness.

Jesus has solved all these problems for you so you can become a tree of righteousness to the glory of God. He has already solved every problem you could ever face. Now you face a choice. Will you live according to Jesus' solutions to your problems?

You see, this is what you have to remember:

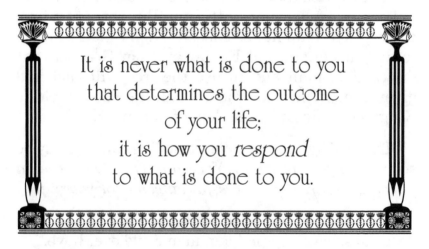

It is never what is done to you that determines the outcome of your life; it is how you *respond* to what is done to you.

When you determine to live by the reality of who you are in Christ, you cannot be controlled by other people's wrong actions or words. Instead, you wake up every morning with the problem-solver's mentality. You tell yourself: *I am going to solve every problem that comes before me today. I'm not going to log it. I'm not going to sit around and think about it. I'm going to solve it. I'm going to look for problems to solve for people so their lives will be better than if they had never met me!*

How does all this apply to the workplace? Let me spell it out for you:

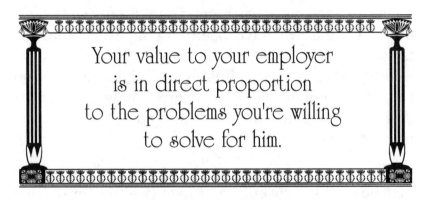

Your value to your employer is in direct proportion to the problems you're willing to solve for him.

Whether people smile or frown when we walk into a room is in direct proportion to the problems we solve. People will either think, *Here comes a solution*, or they'll think, *Oh, no — here comes that problem again!*

You see, we are either solving problems or creating problems every day of our lives. We cannot be neutral. Thus, this next principle is a fact of life:

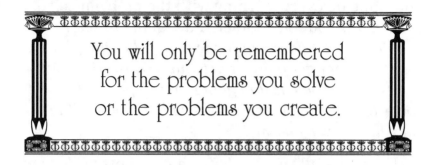

You will only be remembered
for the problems you solve
or the problems you create.

If we would sit back and evaluate our past performance at our jobs, more than likely we would discover that we have been solving less problems than we thought we were. If so, we need to start making the needed adjustments right away. You see, the moment we create more problems than we solve, we have put ourselves in a position to become unnecessary.

For instance, if a person has a chronic bad attitude in the workplace, it is only a matter of time before he is replaced. He has now lit the fuse on the outcome of his position in that job. How can I say that? It's very simple. It is unnatural for a businessperson to maintain a painful relationship. As soon as he can find someone who will do the job with no pain, he will get rid of the painful relationship.

So to become a problem-*solver* instead of a problem-*creator*, follow this advice:

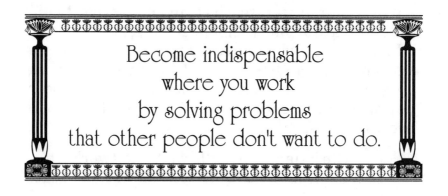

Become indispensable
where you work
by solving problems
that other people don't want to do.

Take on the tasks other people don't want, and do the work better than anyone else can do it.

Employees like that are so rare. The truth is, about 83 percent of the population cannot work without direct oversight. They have to have someone looking over their shoulder eight hours a day. Another 14 percent need some oversight. So if you are a problem-solver, you have nowhere to go but up in the company or business you work for!

I believe the number-one truth left out of most prosperity teaching in the Body of Christ today is this:

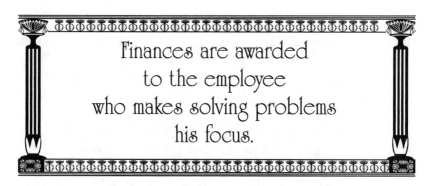

Finances are awarded
to the employee
who makes solving problems
his focus.

When a minister teaches about prosperity, he needs to teach about problem-solving, because that is the means by which prosperity comes. This is the reason millions and millions of Christians hear prosperity teaching week after week and still stay poor. They have never learned to solve the problem that is closest to them.

Some Christians say, "I want to work in a Christian environment." But why do they say that?

If I were you, I'd rather work in a lost environment because it gives you the opportunity to walk out your Christian life in front of people who don't know the success principles you know. Opportunity for advancement is easy because there is rarely any competition in problem-solving. It's a cinch!

Everyone will think you're a fool because you're constantly looking for ways to serve and help the people around you. But in the end, they'll see the reward for a problem-solver is promotion and prosperity!

You Are Not
Your Own Problem-Solver

The sad truth is, most people are *not* problem-solvers. Some have no success in this arena because they expect life to revolve around themselves. Their entire focus is on doing whatever it takes to get other people to solve *their* problems.

These are often the people who beg to be in a union. You see, unions actually came into existence because people wanted to be mediocre — not just the workers, but also the owners. They both wanted something, and they were going to do everything they had to do in order to get it.

People say, "No, I want to be in the union because I can make more money that way."

But that isn't the real reason. Most people want to be in a union because they never learned how to become problem-solvers themselves.

Many great men and women have been disqualified because of their refusal to walk the road of problem-solving. God cannot promote a person unless he is solving someone else's problems. You see, whatever help that person is unwilling to give to others is the same help he will one day need himself.

It boils down to this: You can't accomplish very much in your life if you don't have someone solving problems for you. You need people who truly have a heart for your success and who desire to be what you need them to be in your life. Without these problem-solvers, you'll go around and around the same mountain again and again, never advancing very far at all.

This next principle explains why this is true:

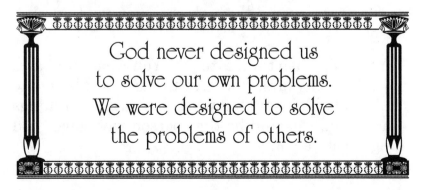

God never designed us
to solve our own problems.
We were designed to solve
the problems of others.

The Good You Do for Others, God Will Do for You

Let's go back to Ephesians 6:8 now and look at it in the context of problem-solving:

Knowing that whatever good anyone does, he will receive the same from the Lord, whether he is a slave or free.

The basic principle set forth in this verse is as follows:

Whatever good we do for another, God will cause to happen for us.

Notice that the apostle Paul did *not* say, "Whatever you do in the life of another, another *man* will do in your life." Paul said that *God* is the One who make things happen for you, even though His blessings may come through the avenue of another person.

You see, it isn't a matter of "You wash my back, and I'll wash yours. You give to me, and I'll give to you." Paul didn't say that when you gave good things to a person, it would be that person who gave good things back to you.

158

That reminds me of a custom many people have in my part of the country when they get married. They keep a log of how much money people give to them as a wedding gift. Then if any of the people who gave them monetary gifts get married in the future, the couple gives that same amount of money back to them as a gift.

That's not what Ephesians 6:8 is talking about. Paul said *God* would give good things back to you, not the person for whom you have just solved a problem.

Meanwhile, the Golden Rule found in Luke 6:31 applies to you: **"And just as you want men to do to you, you also do to them likewise."** How do you want to be treated? That's the way you should treat others. Even when other people refuse to solve your problems, you can determine to solve theirs and receive blessings from God in return.

Notice also the end of Ephesians 6:8: **"...whether he is a slave or free."** That means it doesn't really matter what your social or economic status is — it doesn't matter whether you're at the top of the ladder or on the bottom rung. You will receive back the good things you do for others because God is the One who will bring those good things into your life.

The world may want to hold you down. People may tell you that you're not going to make it. But it doesn't matter what anyone says or does to you; the fact remains that as you solve problems for others, your prosperity and your promotion come from the Lord.

So here's the principle you can use as a measuring stick to evaluate your performance in the workplace:

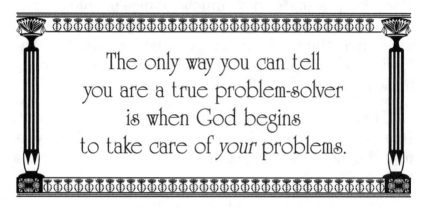

The only way you can tell you are a true problem-solver is when God begins to take care of *your* problems.

No One Can Stop God From Promoting a Problem-Solver

You may be thinking, *Yes, but I've done a lot for my employer, and it hasn't helped at all. He's just standing in my way, keeping me from being promoted.*

Friend, let me help you here with another principle:

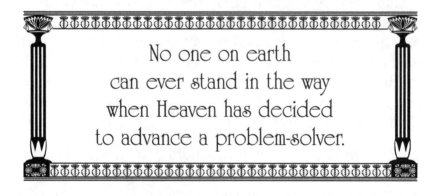

No one on earth can ever stand in the way when Heaven has decided to advance a problem-solver.

You have to get that fact planted deep in your heart. *No one can stop you!* People may want to set

160

up roadblocks to keep you from moving upward, but you'll just sidestep those roadblocks and keep on rising to the next level!

Now, it's true that God never designed you to fix your own problems; He designed others to fix your problems. But since that is true, there is only one way you can keep from getting resentful and offended when others refuse to solve problems for you.

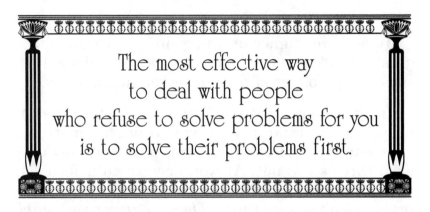

The most effective way to deal with people who refuse to solve problems for you is to solve their problems first.

Even lost society understands the idea, "If you do something for me, I'll do something for you." That's the way the world does business. But God takes that idea about 85 more steps up the ladder when He says, "Whatever you do for others, I will make the same thing happen for you"!

Here is another important point to understand along this line:

161

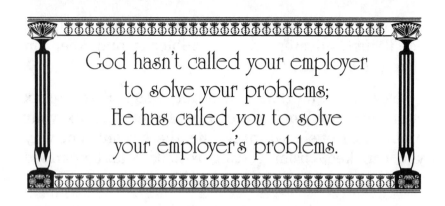

God hasn't called your employer to solve your problems; He has called *you* to solve your employer's problems.

In fact, the higher up you go in your vocation, the greater capacity you will gain to understand and help solve the problems of those over you in authority.

So get ahold of this fact: It doesn't matter if people try to stand in your way. It doesn't matter if your employer disappoints you, puts you down, or even throws you out. All you need to do is focus on your relationship with God and continue to be a problem-solver for others. *Then whatever you make happen for others, God will make happen for you!*

What It Means To Be a Servant

The day I learned that particular lesson was the day I learned the greatest lesson of my life. I had already learned how to be a servant. In fact, serving has always come naturally to me, so it wasn't any big deal to learn how to serve others. But then I learned that I had to take it up another notch: I had to adopt a lifestyle of problem-solving for others.

The same will be true in your life. God will teach you first servanthood and then problem-solving.

Here's the reason you can't reverse the order of these two stages in your walk with Him:

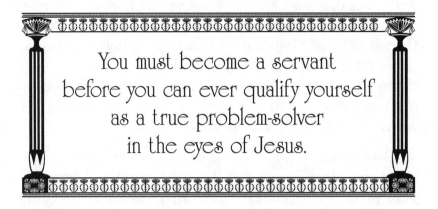

You must become a servant before you can ever qualify yourself as a true problem-solver in the eyes of Jesus.

Problem-solving will usher you into God's will for your life more quickly than any other known quality, and the fastest way to problem-solving is to first become a servant.

But how do you know when God views you as a servant? Let's look at what Jesus said in Mark 10 about this subject:

But Jesus called them to Himself and said to them, "You know that those who are considered rulers over the Gentiles lord it over them, and their great ones exercise authority over them.

"Yet it shall not be so among you; but whoever desires to become great among you shall be your servant."

Mark 10:42,43

163

In verse 42, Jesus talks about the way it is in the world's system, where people obey their authorities only because they want to avoid the negative consequences they'll experience if they don't. People know that if they act contrary to their employer's wishes, their employer will then exercise his lordship over them with negative consequences, such as the loss of a paycheck or even their job. That's how people are controlled in the workplace.

But Jesus said, "It shall not be so among you believers. If you want to be great in My Kingdom, you have to learn to be a servant." Jesus was saying that the more you grow into greatness with God, the more you enlarge your capacity to serve people with a right heart. Therefore, you don't have to be controlled by fear of consequences; instead, you serve others because it has become a genuine inner desire.

So once you choose to be a servant, how can you know if you have become a servant in God's eyes? Just use this guideline:

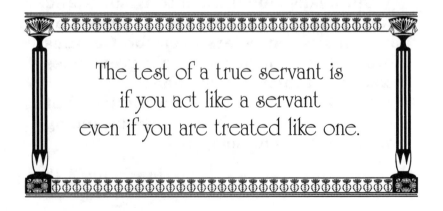

The test of a true servant is
if you act like a servant
even if you are treated like one.

When most people are treated in an ill manner, they retract their willingness to serve. They say, "I'm not going to serve you anymore because of the way you spoke to me" or "You did this to me, so I'm through serving you!"

Refuse To Take Offense

Early in my Christian walk, I asked God to change my character for the better every day. I knew I wasn't the person I needed to be yet, but I was headed in the right direction — I wanted to be a person of excellence. And although I had a long way to go, at least I was willing to change.

One of the ways God answered my prayer for change was to bring a person into my life who had no real friends. I became the best friend this man had ever had in his entire life — and we weren't really even friends! My relationship with this man reminded me more of a boxer in training — with me as the punching bag!

It wasn't easy to take what that person had to dish out to me every time I saw him. But I remember the day something clicked in my mind, causing me to determine, *I absolutely refuse to get offended over anything this man or anyone else ever says or does to me!*

I learned a principle that day that will greatly help you in the workplace if you'll just put it into practice:

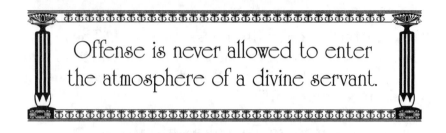

Offense is never allowed to enter the atmosphere of a divine servant.

Sometimes we actually need people in our lives who aren't easy to deal with. I know I did. Of course, when I was living through my difficult relationships, I didn't think I needed those people. But as I look back on those times, I know now that I wouldn't be able to stand strong in the face of adversity the way I have if I hadn't had people in my life teaching me not to get offended when everything was going relatively smoothly.

In every one of those relationships, God promoted me as I kept a servant's heart. But if I had responded negatively, it could have cost me everything.

You just can't afford to take offense in the workplace. If strife and resentment begin to govern the way you relate to your employer or your coworkers, that offense could end up costing you more than you'll ever know.

People say, "Oh, I just blew up and got angry that one time. It's no big deal, but I'm sorry."

You know, sometimes "sorry" just doesn't make it. If we're going to be people of excellence in the workplace, we must continually filter our outgoing communication. Then instead of doing the damage and afterward saying, "Oh, I'm sorry," we'll be able to say, "Before I took offense and had a fit of anger, I decided not to do it"!

Become What Your Employer Wants You To Be

Serving *others* has one very noticeable effect: It changes *you*.

When I first started learning how to be a servant, one pastor said to me, "I'll tell you what, Robb. You say you're a servant?"

"Yes sir," I answered.

"All right," he said. "Then you be here at five o'clock."

I said, "Yes, Sir" — and I was there right on time at five o'clock. The pastor couldn't believe it, but I was just operating in this principle of servanthood:

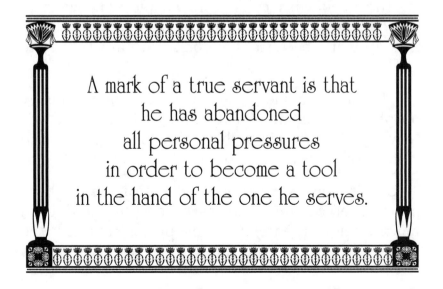

A mark of a true servant is that
he has abandoned
all personal pressures
in order to become a tool
in the hand of the one he serves.

You may say, "But you don't know the pressures and problems I'm dealing with. How do I just unload them before I come to work and become what my employer wants me to be?"

I realize those problems may seem big to you. However, the true size of the problems you face is relative to the position you hold in life.

I remember a minister friend telling me what his little sister once said to him (she was in the third grade at the time): "You think *you* owe money! My life is over! I owe someone at school *42 cents!*"

Problems indeed seem big or small depending on the position you occupy in life. For instance, Ecclesiastes 5:11 says, **"When goods increase, they increase who eat them...."** In other words, the more money you have, the more people will try to take it away from you. If you don't have your phone ringing off the hook with calls from people who want to borrow money from you, that means you don't have this problem, because you don't have any money to lend!

The more money you have, the more money people will be asking for. Deciding when to give and to whom can be a big problem, because the devil will always try to cause you to give to the unqualified.

So although your problems seem huge, make a practice of casting your cares on the Lord each morning as you enter the workplace. Then ask the Holy Spirit to give you the wisdom to serve well as you become what your employer needs you to be for that day.

Characteristics of a True Servant

Now with all this in mind, let's talk about the characteristics of a true servant.

1. A TRUE SERVANT EMBRACES THE TIMES THAT PEOPLE TAKE HIM TO HIS PROVING GROUND.

This is the way to keep from becoming a casualty in the workplace. When someone leads you to your testing ground, don't run from the situation. Instead, *embrace* it as an opportunity to pass another test.

Eventually you'll start recognizing when someone is leading you to your testing ground, but at first it's difficult to do that. You just think people are invading your life in a way they have no right to do. You may think the requests being made to you are greater than anything that should ever be asked of any person. You may even think, *How dare my employer ask me to do that! I know I wanted to be a servant, but I never thought he would require me to do this!*

I can think of several prominent Christians who failed the test when they were led in this way to their testing ground — and no one has heard of them since. They faded into obscurity because they refused to maintain a servant's heart.

You see, friend, you have to understand:

169

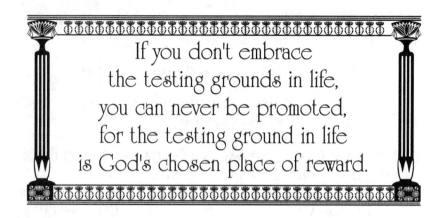

If you don't embrace
the testing grounds in life,
you can never be promoted,
for the testing ground in life
is God's chosen place of reward.

Personally, I *want* to be taken to my proving ground. I want to be taken to a place where someone I respect sits me down and says, "Now, you really need to be taking care of this responsibility" or "You really need to make this change."

I recall a time recently when a man I submit my life to sat me down and began to set the stage for a serious discussion. When I discovered what he was doing, I politely interrupted him and said, "Respectfully, Sir, you are not required to beat around the bush. Please tell me exactly what you want me to do, and it will be done before the sun goes down." It would not even matter to me if that individual did not care for me, for I will never allow someone's disregard of me stand in the way of my promotion.

Developing a servant's heart is not a game and it is not for the faint-hearted or the easily offended. Think about it — people around the world today are losing their lives by mentioning the Name of Jesus once. Yet Christians are getting offended in the

170

American workplace because they don't like it when their employer asks them to do something they don't want to do!

You may as well get ready, because you *will* be tested in your character on your way to becoming a true servant. Otherwise, God will never be able to trust you with the true riches of His Kingdom.

2. A TRUE SERVANT IS DILIGENT.

Proverbs 10:4 says, **"He who has a slack hand becomes poor, but the hand of the diligent makes rich."** Why is this promise important to you? Because in order to become all that God wants you to be, you will have to have money. Finances are necessary in order to fulfill what God has called you to do. However, you have to go about obtaining that wealth *God's* way — the way of diligent servant-hood.

To maintain a diligent attitude at work, always focus on this question: *What benefit does my employer receive from his relationship with me?* That kind of attitude will reap a great harvest for you that can never be obtained by asking, *What am I getting out of all this hard work I'm doing for my employer?*

3. A TRUE SERVANT IS FAITHFUL.

We've already talked about this quality in regard to the pursuit of excellence in the workplace. But let me stress this point:

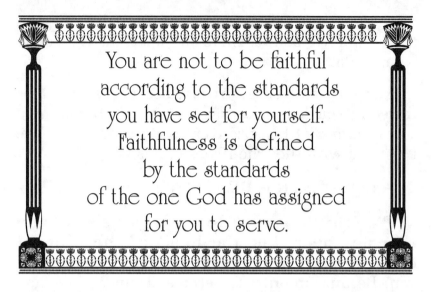

You are not to be faithful according to the standards you have set for yourself. Faithfulness is defined by the standards of the one God has assigned for you to serve.

In First Corinthians 4:2, the Bible says, **"Moreover it is required in stewards that one be found faithful."** In your job, you are a steward or a servant to one or more people. And to that person or persons, you *must* be faithful — not according to your standard, but according to the standards of those God has placed over you.

We don't need someone on the sidelines saying, "You poor thing — you do more than you should do at your job. Your employer should never ask you to do all that." God doesn't judge how faithful we are according to others' standards; God judges our faithfulness according to the standards of those He has placed over us.

That's why this principle is so important:

172

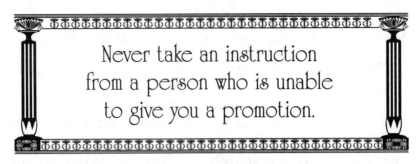

Never take an instruction
from a person who is unable
to give you a promotion.

We should never have our ear glued to a person who can't promote us after he is finished telling us his perspective of life. On the other hand, it's also important for us to understand this:

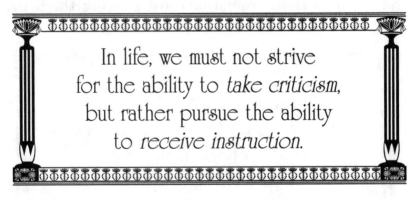

In life, we must not strive
for the ability to *take criticism*,
but rather pursue the ability
to *receive instruction*.

Why must we learn to receive instruction? Because that is the only way we will be counted faithful by the standards of those in authority over us. When we consistently receive and act on our authority's instructions, we don't have to keep taking correction for the same mistake again and again. Instruction received and acted upon prevents the next time of correction from ever coming.

Some people never learn from their mistakes, nor do they ever learn how to receive the instruction they need to change. About the third or fourth time around the block, they tell their authority, "You never treat me right when it comes to this issue."

"Well, you just need to change in that area of your life."

"I don't care — you still shouldn't treat me that way!" But how do these people expect correction to come? They should search the Scriptures to find out how God treats people who are disobedient, unwilling, and unfaithful!

People who are not faithful are often upset when they realize that promotions are passing them by. They need to recognize this principle:

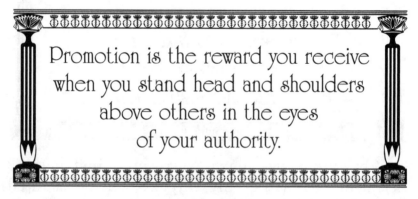

Promotion is the reward you receive when you stand head and shoulders above others in the eyes of your authority.

If someone isn't serving his superior on the job with a servant's heart — if he isn't looking for problems to solve for the person to whom God has assigned him — it becomes easy to predict the result. That person cannot be promoted. As we saw before, money is a reward for solving the problems of others.

174

Fortunately, even though we may have been stuck in a place of no promotion, we don't have to stay there. If we don't like the results we are living with today, we can just determine to change our actions. Whatever we don't like, we can change.

Now, I'm a quick learner. All you need to do is show me what I'm doing wrong. Just show me my "PRD" — my "Position Results Description" — which tells me, "This job will be completed when I successfully accomplish these tasks." I'll leave with my PRD and come back to you with a successfully completed job in record time!

Too many Christians don't want to receive instruction or correction. You almost have to backslide to talk to them because all they want to do is go back to spiritual kindergarten and hear about how good they are.

People spend way too much time thinking about life from their own perspective instead of thinking about it from *God's* perspective. I don't want to do that. I want to see every situation the way God sees it. I want to be counted faithful according to *His* standards. I *don't* want to look back at the end of my life and wish that I had received instruction better so the outcome of my time on this earth could be different.

Let's look at one more characteristic of servanthood — an important one that we've already discussed at length.

4. A TRUE SERVANT IS RESPECTFUL.

Proverbs 28:14 says, **"Happy is the man who is always reverent...."** A servant is respectful. We saw earlier in First Timothy 6:1 (*NIV*) that **"all who are under the yoke of slavery should consider their masters worthy of FULL respect...."** This same principle applies to employees.

Now, that means you are not to give your employer a half-hearted form of respect. You are not to speak one way in front of him and another way behind his back. Paul is talking about giving your employer full respect. That means a 360-degree type of respect that is given 24 hours a day, 7 days a week! Here's one big reason God requires this:

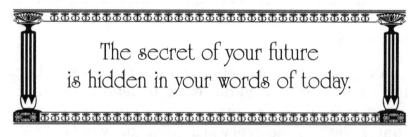

The secret of your future
is hidden in your words of today.

It is impossible for your life to go in a different direction than the words coming out of your mouth because your words are both spirit and eternal. Every word you have ever spoken is carried on the wind of time and reaches into eternity — powerful seed that produces an inevitable harvest in your life, whether good or bad.

- Every disrespectful word you have ever spoken from the time you were a little child is still out there somewhere.

176

- Every commitment you've ever made that you haven't kept is still out there.

- Every vow to God you've ever made that you haven't followed through on is *still out there.*

You can see why it's so important to **"let no corrupt word proceed out of your mouth, but what is good for necessary edification..."** (Eph. 4:29)!

First Timothy 6:1 (*NIV*) goes on to tell you some of the consequences of disrespect:

All who are under the yoke of slavery should consider their masters worthy of full respect, so that God's name and our teaching may not be slandered.

Do you realize whose reputation gets hurt when a Christian doesn't act like a believer in the workplace? *God's* reputation. That person's coworkers know he's a Christian, so they watch him when he takes time away from his supervisor at the water cooler. They see this Christian when he gossips about his supervisor or laughs when others joke about him.

A Christian employee's disrespect actually slanders the name of God, mocks the teaching of God's Word, and neuters his Christian witness. Respect is indeed a serious matter, required in order to fulfill First Timothy 6:1: **"...that the name of God and His doctrine may not be blasphemed."**

However, a person's disrespect of the past doesn't have to harm his future. He can change his disrespectful attitudes and the wrong ways he has thought and spoken by developing a servant's heart.

So don't dwell on the wrong words and actions of days gone by. You can't keep dodging your past if you want to go on to a higher level in God.

Sometimes in order to have clear sailing as a servant, you have to let go of your past mistakes and failures. Otherwise, those mistakes will take you through the meteor shower of Satan's disappointment and distraction and keep you from achieving what God has for you in the days ahead.

That never has to happen to you, friend. Just remember:

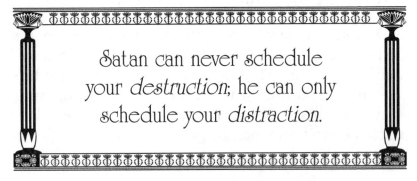

Satan can never schedule your *destruction*; he can only schedule your *distraction*.

Characteristics of a Bad Servant

Obviously, disrespect is one character quality of a bad servant. Let's look at a few other characteristics of bad servants that the Bible sets forth.

1. A BAD SERVANT IS **IDLE.**

A bad servant is a person who doesn't even complete his basic responsibilities. On the job, his work area is unkempt and disorganized. He spends too much time around the water cooler chatting with coworkers and not enough time doing what he is supposed to do!

This person fits the description of a bad servant in Proverbs 18:9 (*KJV*): **"He also that is slothful in his work is brother to him that is a great waster."**

This is the reason you don't find any of my clothes lying around on the floor in my home. Not one piece of clothing is out of its place where I live. I don't have the attitude, "Oh, this is our house; I can just act any way I want to." No, I can't act any way I want to. My home is *God's* house. He's paying for it.

Some people might protest, "Are you saying I can't be a slob anywhere?" That's what I'm saying. If someone wants to be a pig, there are places where pigs are kept called pigpens!

"Well, I'm just not very tidy." But anyone can learn how to be tidy if he wants to make the effort.

"But I like to keep all my papers in piles on my desk. That way I know exactly where everything is."

Actually, what these people really like to do is stay idle when they should be busy organizing and cleaning up their work area!

2. A BAD SERVANT IS **DISHONEST.**

Jesus said in Luke 16:10 (*NIV*), **"Whoever can be trusted with very little can also be trusted with much...."** That's a good scripture for us to remember the next time we're tempted to talk on the telephone with a friend during company time or take some pens and paper clips home from the office for our own personal use!

Jesus said if a person isn't an honest and a trustworthy servant in the little things, he won't be able to be trusted with the big things. That's why dishonesty is a big reason many people never rise to the next level in the workplace.

3. A BAD SERVANT IS **DISLOYAL.**

Disloyalty is a horrible thing. It can break the heart of a mentor when someone whom God has called to serve him says, "I don't want this relationship anymore. I'm checking out!"

In Luke 16:13, Jesus addresses this quality of disloyalty when He said, **"No servant can serve two masters...."** In part, Jesus' message was this: *"Disloyalty will disqualify you."*

4. A BAD SERVANT IS **ARGUMENTATIVE.**

The account we read earlier in Acts 23:1-5 addresses this subject. When the apostle Paul was brought before the Jewish council, the High Priest said to the guard, "Smack him one." So the guard smacked him, and Paul responded in anger, "God is going to smack you, you white-washed wall!"

Then the person next to Paul said to him, "Do you dare revile God's high priest?"

180

Paul immediately responded, "I didn't know he was the high priest. If I had known, I never would have said that."

Paul understood that he was never to allow his speech to become free regarding any authority figure. An argumentative servant is a bad servant, and Paul had a true servant's heart.

A Bad Servant
Can Change for the Better

Fortunately, a bad servant can change to become a *good* servant. We see this in the example of John Mark, a young man whom God had called to serve Paul and Barnabus in the ministry.

Barnabus was Paul's sidekick, a man of God who really ministered to Paul in his life. Barnabas served as Paul's mentor in the early days of his ministry, taking Paul under his wing and teaching him everything he knew. However, as sometimes happens in the ministry, the protégé — in this case, Paul — eventually became the mentor.

Even then, the apostles Paul and Barnabas were an inseparable duo. They had a strong commitment to one another because they knew that two are better than one on the frontlines of ministry. The prayer of agreement can be prayed. The two can walk through difficult circumstances together instead of alone.

There came a time when Paul and Barnabas decided to take along a young man named John Mark on their missionary travels. However, as it turned out, John Mark just wasn't ready for the difficulties and the testings they encountered along the way; he wasn't qualified to maintain that level of ministry yet. So he decided to leave Paul and Barnabas and return home in the middle of their journey.

But Barnabus wouldn't relent. Barnabus continued his relationship with John Mark, even though the younger man had abandoned them at an inopportune time. And even though John Mark wasn't qualified to be in a servant's relationship with the two apostles any longer, Barnabas wanted to take him along with them on the next journey. Paul emphatically opposed such a request.

Finally, the schism between the two apostles became so hurtful that Barnabus went his way with John Mark and Paul went a different direction with someone he could trust — a young man named Silas (*see* Acts 15:36-40).

But something happened between that time and the time Paul wrote his second letter to Timothy. At this point, Paul's life was almost over. All his epistles had been written, and he had come to his last hours on this earth. Yet he said, **"Only Luke is with me. Take Mark, and bring him with thee: for he is profitable to me for the ministry"** (2 Tim. 4:11 *KJV*).

Why was John Mark now profitable to Paul for the ministry? Because the younger man had turned around and requalified himself!

Friend, it doesn't matter where you are right now in your job. It doesn't matter if you are currently disqualified from being called a true servant. Just remember — the way you go from disqualification to where God wants you to be is to *requalify*. And how do you do that?

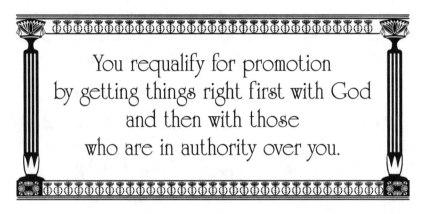

You requalify for promotion by getting things right first with God and then with those who are in authority over you.

We must rekindle the relationships that open the doors of opportunity by becoming first true servants and then problem-solvers. This is God's way of promoting us — of bringing us into His highest so we can fully carry out all He has called us to do in our jobs.

I don't know about you, but I'm thankful that I determined never to quit in the areas of my life where I had once disqualified myself. I never said it was too late to keep trying; I never threw in the towel; and I never for a moment accused those who spoke words of correction into my life of being wrong. I just kept pursuing excellence until I had requalified myself to be a true servant of God in every area of my life.

That has to be your determination as well if you're going to receive the promotions God has in store for you. To enter into the fullness of God's plan for you in the workplace, there will be certain interior issues of character you will have to deal with. But if you will refuse to give up — if you will keep on going until every hindrance is discovered and destroyed — *nothing* can stand in your way of becoming all God intends for you to become!

You Choose Your Own Consequences

That's my continual confession: *I cannot be stopped!* I simply won't allow anything to get in the way of my pursuit toward excellence. I make this my guiding principle in life:

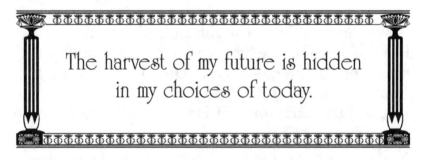

The harvest of my future is hidden
in my choices of today.

It's one thing to make a mistake. It's another thing to make a wrong choice. God forgives mistakes, but we live with our choices. That's why we must always keep this in mind:

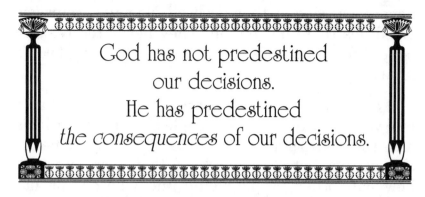

God has not predestined
our decisions.
He has predestined
the consequences of our decisions.

The decision to walk in disrespect can result in some of the most serious consequences of all. In fact, I would go so far as to state it this way:

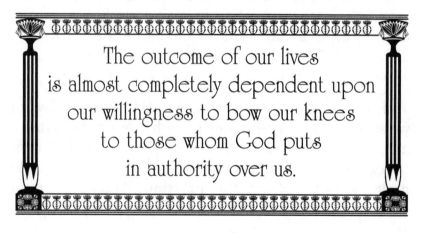

The outcome of our lives
is almost completely dependent upon
our willingness to bow our knees
to those whom God puts
in authority over us.

Consider this: More than 90 percent of the people you go to work with every day don't like their job. They have a poor attitude, and they are waiting for someone on whom they can unload their poor attitude.

These people have no idea what it means to have a servant's heart, nor do they care to know. They are always misunderstood for some reason. They are never rewarded as they deserve. No one encourages or edifies them on the job. They never receive any benefit from their jobs — and it's all their employer's fault.

I don't believe any of that is true. Everyone has a free will, so why are those people allowing their lives and their attitudes to be determined by someone else at their jobs? If they have their own free will, how can other people determine whether or not they're going to be happy with their work?

The truth is, the outcome of our lives is based on the decisions we make. We can actually choose our own consequences. Therefore, we can't blame our unhappiness or our bad attitudes in the workplace on others. Whether or not we receive the rewards of servanthood at our jobs depends entirely on *us*.

I no longer think only from the perspective of whether or not a decision is right or wrong. Now I always take the time to evaluate what kind of consequences will result from the decision I'm about to make. I try to answer the question, *What is going to happen if I do this?*

To become people of excellence, we must begin to train ourselves this way as well. We must learn to live our lives for long-term rather than short-term gratification. In other words, we must pay the price now to enjoy the greatest benefits later. We must embrace short-term pain in order to enjoy long-term pleasure.

When we make a decision that gives us nothing but immediate, short-term gratification, we may pay for that short-term gratification for the rest of our lives. That wrong decision could start us down a road that leaves us marred and scarred in the end.

That's why it's so important for us to understand that our lives are completely determined by the decisions we make because those decisions have pre-determined outcomes. For instance, suppose we get up tomorrow morning and decide we don't want to do a good job at work that day. That is our choice — but we better be ready for our employer to say, "You need to pick up your severance check because we don't need you anymore!"

You can rest assured — there is nothing hidden that won't be revealed. The Bible says it like this: **"...Be sure your sin will find you out"** (Num. 32:23).

A person won't have any problem getting in trouble on the job if that's what he wants to do. But when he loses favor with his employer, he shouldn't start asking, "Why did God let this happen to me?" God *didn't* let it happen. That person just made a decision that carried a predetermined consequence!

Recently a young business owner expressed to me how thankful she was for my input into her new business. However, she told me, she was dealing with one particular challenge: With all the new business that was coming in, she was having a difficult time focusing.

I responded with these words: "Don't even think about it. If you don't find the resolve to focus on the new business God has given to you, it won't be long before you won't have to deal with that challenge anymore, because the new business will stop coming in!"

I was just letting this business owner know what we all need to understand: The outcome of her business endeavor will depend on whether or not she embraces short-term pain in order to enjoy long-term pleasure.

Principles of Promotion

It's easy to understand why so many people go unrewarded in the workplace. They just don't do the necessary things to be rewarded.

You see, although life is designed to be a continual ascension, most people stopped ascending long ago. They just exist now at their jobs, doing what they're supposed to do by rote. What is the root of their condition? Somewhere along the line, they stopped trying to solve the problems of those to whom they were assigned.

You can't do that if you want to be promoted at your job. You have to continually press into problem-solving. You have to ask yourself constantly, *What problems can I solve for my employer today? What can I do to make his life easier?*

In fact, take it one step further:

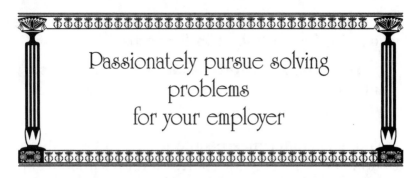

Passionately pursue solving problems for your employer

By staying ahead of the inevitable (when the problem is actually assigned to you), you can make the problem work for you by solving it beforehand. In fact, the problem may even get you a promotion!

Think about it — why would you want to wait to solve a certain problem when you know that you will eventually have to deal with it anyway? So if you see the problem coming, stay ahead of the game. Start solving that problem before it sneaks up behind you and smacks you on the head, turning your entire schedule upside down as you try to fix it.

This next principle goes along with the last one. It's another vital key in your passionate pursuit to solve problems in the workplace:

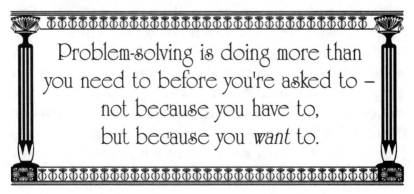

Problem-solving is doing more than you need to before you're asked to – not because you have to, but because you *want* to.

We can find another reason people go unrewarded in the workplace in Proverbs 3:27:

Do not withhold good from those to whom it is due, when it is in the power of your hand to do so.

You see, sometimes people try to solve problems at their job that are not theirs to fix because it isn't in the power of their hand to do it. Or they spend all their time trying to solve problems for the unqualified, or for those to whom it is not due. Then they wonder why they're not seeing multiplication in this area of their lives!

Second Thessalonians 3:10,11 talks about one category of the unqualified you will probably encounter in the workplace:

For even when we were with you, we commanded you this: If anyone will not work, neither shall he eat.
For we hear that there are some who walk among you in a disorderly manner, not working at all, but are busybodies.

If you look around, you will more than likely find people at your job who are busybodies. These people tend to infect everyone else with their negative words of gossip and complaint. They always want to let you know about their aches and pains or what someone else did to offend them. Whatever useless tidbit of information they have to give, it usually only makes the situation worse when you listen and sympathize.

People who waste most of their time trying to solve the problems of the unqualified don't understand the truth of this biblical principle:

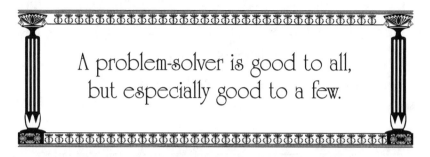

A problem-solver is good to all, but especially good to a few.

This principle is found in Galatians 6:10, which tells us, **"Therefore, as we have opportunity, let us do good to all, especially to those who are of the household of faith."** The problem-solver is good to everyone, but exclusivity is important to him. He kicks it up a notch when it comes to solving problems for the people to whom God has assigned him.

When I relate to those whom God has placed over me in the Lord, I want to know, "Where am I on your list of problem-solvers in your life? Am I number six? Number eight? Number nine? Because if you tell me I'm number nine, you give me something to shoot for. I'll go after the goal of becoming your number-one problem-solver! Just bring me anything that no one else wants to do, and you'll find the task completed before the sun goes down!"

Here's another principle that will help you attain that higher level you seek in the workplace:

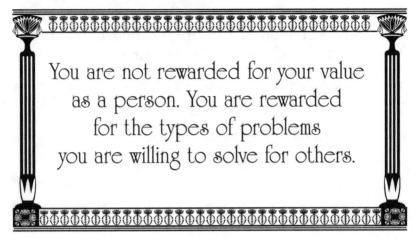

You are not rewarded for your value as a person. You are rewarded for the types of problems you are willing to solve for others.

The person who cleans the bathrooms may very well be a wonderful person, and I thank God for such people! Where would we be without them? But as long as cleaning bathrooms is the problem this person has chosen to solve with his life, his choice determines that he will live within the means of a limited amount of finances. He won't go far beyond that level of wages until he begins to solve a higher level of problems for someone else.

One person is a secretary and earns $8.00 an hour. Another person is an attorney, and his clients pay him $300.00 an hour. Why is this? The reason is not that the attorney is nicer than the secretary. It is just that the attorney has chosen to solve a greater problem. The type of problems a person solves for others determines the amount for which he is recompensed for his labor.

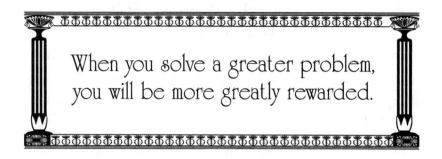

When you solve a greater problem, you will be more greatly rewarded.

For instance, if an employee wants a raise, his employer has the right to ask him, "What new kinds of problems are you going to solve for me that warrant more money than you're making right now?" That rationale makes a lot more sense than an employee who says, "Well, everyone else in the office gets a raise in January, so I want one too."

This brings us to one principle of problem-solving along this line:

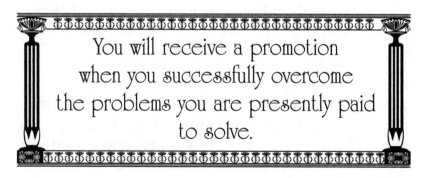

You will receive a promotion when you successfully overcome the problems you are presently paid to solve.

In other words, you will be rewarded when you deserve it according to God's principles of promotion.

Don't Reject the Problem-Solvers In Your Life

Do you know what you need if you want to get in position to advance to the next level in the workplace? You need problem-solvers who are called to help you.

There are so few true problem-solvers in the Body of Christ. I thank God for every one of them, especially the ones whom God has called to take me to the woodshed every now and then! When these people visit me, we don't sit around exchanging small talk. We get right down to business, talking about what needs to change in my life.

Sometimes it isn't easy to sit through those conversations. There are times I come out feeling like I've just been through a meat grinder! But I wouldn't have it any other way. I want to reach the finish line in becoming all God intends for me to be, and He has called these problem-solvers to help me get there.

You see, we don't need someone to be there for us at the beginning of the race nearly as much as we need someone at the end of the race. At the starting gate, we're looking good with our leg warmers and our workout outfits. The Holy Spirit takes good care of us. He draws us to read the Bible and even shows us what to read.

But by the end of the race, we aren't running in a pack with the other runners anymore; we're all just straggling in one by one. In fact, most of the runners around us aren't even making it to the end of the race!

(As I said earlier, most people are good starters, but very few are good finishers. Most are very good at starting project after project after project. But it seems that almost every time they get in the middle of something, they get distracted, lose interest, get bored with it, and quit.)

Meanwhile, we're just trying to get our exhausted bodies across the finish line. This is the time we can make the most mistakes if we don't have problem-solvers along the sidelines, cheering us on and guiding us along the way.

Let's look at an example in the Bible of someone who not only recognized the person God had placed in her life to guide her, but who was willing to become that person's problem-solver. The woman's name was Ruth.

Ruth and Orpah were two Moabite women who had married Israelite brothers named Mahlon and Chilion. These brothers and their parents, Elimelech and Naomi, had moved to Moab when things got tough in Israel during a time of famine. But calamity later hit the family when the three men of the family all died within a short period of time. Naomi was left alone in a foreign land with her two pagan daughter-in-laws.

In her grief, Naomi made the decision to return to her homeland, for she had heard that the famine was over in Israel. She told her daughter-in-laws,

"Girls, I have no more to give you. Even if I gave birth to another son today, you'd still have to wait for him to grow up and become a man who could take care of you. You should go back to your own families and your own god. Go back to where there is comfort and the prospect of new husbands."

Orpah had no problem with Naomi's request. With no more men left to marry in Naomi's household, she found it very reasonable to kiss Naomi good-bye and leave. Although this must have been difficult for Orpah, self-preservation spoke louder than loyalty to her.

But Ruth's response was completely different. She said, "Uh, uh — I'm not going!"

"But I don't have anything left to give you!" Naomi protested. "My life is over. I'm impoverished. I don't have a dime."

"I don't care," Ruth said. "I'm coming with you anyway. Wherever you go, whatever you do, I'm committed to you. Your God will take care of us."

Sadly, many Christians admire Ruth but live the life of Orpah. They are continually on the receiving end, happy as long as everything is going their way. But the minute something bad happens, they have sour grapes all over town! They get angry and rebellious and start blaming others for their troubles. Often they just walk away, leaving everyone else to cope with the situation.

But consider Ruth. The Bible says Ruth *clave* unto Naomi (Ruth 1:14 *KJV*). Ruth had no prospect for the future. She had nothing to look forward to. It was just she and a sad old woman — that was it.

Nevertheless, Ruth chose to be a problem-solver in the life of Naomi, saying these words to her:

"...Entreat me not to leave you, or to turn back from following after you; for wherever you go, I will go; and wherever you lodge, I will lodge; your people shall be my people, and your God, my God.

Where you die, I will die, and there will I be buried. The Lord do so to me, and more also, if anything but death parts you and me."

Ruth 1:16,17

In other words, Ruth was saying to Naomi, "May it go worse in my life than this if I ever walk away from you and what you are experiencing right now."

You know, all of us long to hear those words from someone. Yet even when we do hear them, we are apprehensive about putting our trust in that person. Many of us have heard those words from people who were more like Orpah than Ruth in our lives!

So the two women traveled to Israel, where Ruth continued to demonstrate wisdom beyond her years or her Moabite background. (After all, she had grown up among people who sacrificed their children to their gods!) Ruth made good on her commitment to Naomi, proving herself to be a comfort to the old woman as she tried to cope with the grief of her loss.

Then all of a sudden from somewhere out in eternity comes this idea about a kinsmen redeemer. Where did that idea come from? It rose up from within Naomi, Ruth's "divine connection."

It all started when Ruth decided to provide food for Naomi by gleaning leftover grain from the fields during harvest time. (According to the Jewish Law, landowners were to leave grain on the fields for the poor to glean.)

One day she was gleaning in the fields of a wealthy landowner named Boaz. Boaz noticed the young woman and asked his servants, "Who is that girl out there?"

"Oh, that's Ruth, Naomi's Moabite daughter-in-law."

Boaz had heard that Ruth was a virtuous woman who was better to Naomi than seven sons and had remained faithful to her mother-in-law through hard times. So he said, "Well, don't any of you men touch her, or you'll deal with me!" Then he told Ruth, "Please stay in my fields to glean, and whenever you need refreshment, feel free to drink the water my laborers bring to the field."

Privately Boaz instructed his servants, "Start dropping some extra grain for Ruth to pick up. Make sure she's well taken care of."

Ruth came home to Naomi that day loaded down with the grain she had gleaned from Boaz's fields. Naomi asked in wonder, "Where did you get all this?"

"I picked it up in Boaz's fields," Ruth replied.

"Boaz!" Naomi exclaimed. "He's our family's kinsman redeemer! God has taken notice of us, and Boaz has taken notice of you."

Now, Boaz was not only unmarried, but he was also a good and honorable man, although quite a bit older than Ruth. So later Naomi said to Ruth, "Let me tell you what you need to do to get a husband. I'm not talking about just any man. I'm going to tell you how to get the best one. If you'll do what I say, it will go well with you."

Now, just consider what would have happened to Ruth if she had said, "You know, I don't want you to talk to me anymore, Naomi. I really appreciate what you've done for me, but I'll take it from here." What would have happened if Ruth had rejected Naomi as her mentor — her God-chosen doorway to her divine destiny?

But Ruth didn't do that. Notice how she responded to Naomi in Ruth 3:5 (*NIV*): **"'I will do whatever you say,' Ruth answered."**

Ruth listened to Naomi as the old woman told her what to do next. "Boaz is going to the threshing floor tonight to winnow all the grain that has been harvested. After he has eaten, he will lie down there to sleep. I want you to go to the threshing floor after he's fallen asleep and lie down at his feet, covering yourself with part of the blanket that covers him. When Boaz wakes up and sees you there, he'll know

199

what to do from there. You won't have to do anything else."

So Ruth went down to the threshing floor that night and did everything her mother-in-law had instructed her to do. She followed Naomi's instructions to the letter!

When Boaz woke up and discovered Ruth lying at his feet, he said, "Bless you, Child, that you would want to serve one such as me when you could have gone after the younger men. You're a virtuous woman.

"However," Boaz continued, "although I am a close relative, there is one man who is closer in relation than I am. You stay here, and I'll go find out if I can take his place as your kinsman redeemer. If so, you will be my bride!'"

Sure as shooting, Ruth became Mrs. Boaz! But that wasn't the end of the story. Even after Ruth married Boaz, Naomi's work in her life wasn't over.

When Ruth's son Obed was born, Naomi's friends proclaimed, "God has wiped away all your shame through your daughter Ruth, who has been better to you than seven sons!" Naomi then became little Obed's nurse, helping Ruth and Boaz nurture and raise him in the fear of the Lord (*see* Ruth 4:14-16). This same Obed would one day grow up to become the father of Jesse and the grandfather of King David.

Think of it — because Ruth was willing to listen to and become a problem-solver for her divine connection, Naomi, she became the great-grandmother of David and one of the ancestors of the Messiah Himself!

Perhaps now you can see why problem-solving is the key that opens the doors of opportunity and success in any area of life, including the workplace. To live a life of continual ascension into God's best, you must not only become a problem-solver for those to whom God has assigned you, but you must embrace those He has assigned to guide you along your way — even when they take you to your most difficult testing ground!

PRINCIPLES FOR BECOMING A PROBLEM SOLVER

★ **Become a person who solves problems in the lives of others.**

★ **It is never what is done to you that determines the outcome of your life; it is how you *respond* to what is done to you.**

★ **Your value to your employer is in direct proportion to the problems you're willing to solve for him.**

★ **You will only be remembered for the problems you solve or the problems you create.**

★ **Become indispensable where you work by solving problems that other people don't want to do.**

★ Finances are awarded to the employee who makes solving problems his focus.

★ God never designed us to solve our own problems. We were designed to solve the problems of others.

★ Whatever good we do for another, God will cause to happen for us.

★ The only way you can tell you are a true problem-solver is when God begins to take care of *your* problems.

★ No one on earth can ever stand in the way when Heaven has decided to advance a problem-solver.

★ The most effective way to deal with people who refuse to solve problems for you is to solve their problems first.

★ God hasn't called your employer to solve your problems; He has called *you* to solve your employer's problems.

★ You must become a servant before you can ever qualify yourself as a true problem-solver in the eyes of Jesus.

★ The test of a true servant is if you act like a servant even if you are treated like one.

★ Offense is never allowed to enter the atmosphere of a divine servant.

★ A mark of a true servant is that he has abandoned all personal pressures in order to become a tool in the hand of the one he serves.

★ If you don't embrace the testing grounds in life, you can never be promoted, for the testing ground in life is God's chosen place of reward.

★ You are not to be faithful according to the standards you have set for yourself. Faithfulness is defined by the standards of the one God has assigned for you to serve.

★ Never take an instruction from a person who is unable to give you a promotion.

★ In life, we must not strive for the ability to *take criticism*, but rather pursue the ability to *receive instruction*.

★ Promotion is the reward you receive when you stand head and shoulders above others in the eyes of your authority.

★ The secret of your future is hidden in your words of today.

★ Satan can never schedule your *destruction*; he can only schedule your *distraction*.

★ You requalify for promotion by getting things right first with God and then with those who are in authority over you.

★ The harvest of my future is hidden in my choices of today.

★ God has not predestined our decisions. He has predestined *the consequences* of our decisions.

★ The outcome of our lives is almost completely dependent upon our willingness to bow our knees to those whom God puts in authority over us.

★ Passionately pursue solving problems for your employer before they become your assignment.

★ Problem-solving is doing more than you need to before you're asked to — not because you have to, but because you want to.

★ A problem-solver is good to all, but especially good to a few.

★ You are not rewarded for your value as a person. You are rewarded for the types of problems you are willing to solve for others.

★ When you solve a greater problem, you will be more greatly rewarded.

★ You will receive a promotion when you successfully overcome the problems you are presently paid to solve.

NOTES:

Notes:

DEVELOPING A SOUND BUSINESS ATTITUDE

If any Christians routinely seem out of place in their position in life, it is the group comprised of Christian business people. So many times these believers struggle with knowing how to reconcile traditional business practices with their Christian beliefs.

But it doesn't have to be that way, and I believe I know what I'm talking about. I understand what it's like to be a Christian businessman because I am involved in business as well as in the ministry.

If you are a business person, I want to specifically address you in this chapter. I have some principles to share with you that will help you develop the biblically sound business attitudes you need to launch your business into a new realm of success, both financially and spiritually.

Over the years, I've found that many Christians who are in business should not be. They don't know the first thing about how to run a successful business. Every time they step out to try a new venture, they fail; and each time, it hurts their faith in themselves and in God a little more.

This is why you need to make sure you are called to do what you are doing as a vocation. You need to make your calling sure so you can be confident that you're following God's best course for your life.

However, if you know you are called to be a Christian business person, I want to show you how to bring the Christian message into the workplace in such a way that it is both palatable and without compromise. You see, there are things you can do as a business person to ensure both continued commerce and a happy work environment. When these principles are practiced, they will bring you success in your business and provide a place for you as a leader in the business community.

The first principle I want to share with you is very basic:

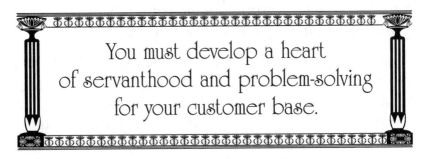

You must develop a heart of servanthood and problem-solving for your customer base.

These are the two virtues that are not a regular part of our everyday lives. Developing these qualities will not only enrich your personal life, but they will also set you apart from the crowd and become your distinction.

Remember, people are the greatest commodity to ever walk the face of the earth. Your potential for developing leadership skills and a heart for people is much more valuable than the potential amount of money you can make. This is the reason:

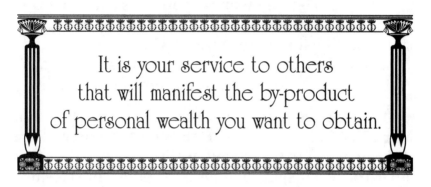

It is your service to others that will manifest the by-product of personal wealth you want to obtain.

Don't rely on negotiating skills and shrewd, sly business strategies to determine how much wealth you are able to accumulate. Instead, allow your servanthood toward people to determine that same goal. Finances (as long as they are honestly gained) is only an indication of the service and the types of problems you are willing to solve for others.

The lack of servanthood in the business realm is one of the greatest problems Christian business people face today, and the root of the problem lies in *wrong attitudes*. Consider this:

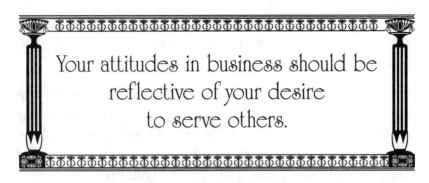

Your attitudes in business should be reflective of your desire to serve others.

Every Christian business person is called by God to be a servant; however, in the everyday routine of running a business, too often a Christian's attitude *doesn't* reflect a desire to serve others. In fact, he may even act as if people owe *him* something.

Jesus stressed the importance of servanthood in Mark 10:45 when He said, **"For even the Son of Man did not come to be served, but to serve...."** The Son of God Himself said, "I'm here to serve." In the same way, you are there to serve people in your industry. It will be very difficult for anyone to reject you when you approach them in humility and say, "I'm here to serve you and to make things better for you."

Remember, money is an indicator of your ability to solve problems for your clientele. That means you can determine the amount of your income. If you're the best at providing your particular service, you will get the work.

Are You an 'Excusiologist'?

To be a successful Christian business person, you have to avoid becoming an "excusiologist." That's a term I coined to define the many Christians I've

210

observed through the years who look for others to blame for their failures.

The excusiologist lives by this categorical lie: "The reason I am in the position I am in is the lack of other people's involvement with me. Others have determined my future for me. They haven't done right by me; therefore, I am a failure based on someone else's actions or lack of action on my behalf."

So take a moment to ask yourself: *Am I a person who makes excuses? Do I spend a lot of time blaming others for my lack of success in my business or career, in my home, or in my relationships?*

Now, you need to understand that there is a difference between an excuse and a reason. An excuse is only an admission of guilt. When you're making excuses for something you have or have not done, you are admitting you're wrong. You're saying in essence, "It really should have been worked out another way, but it wasn't. So here is my excuse for not doing it right."

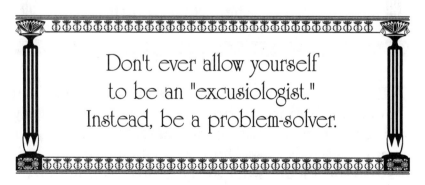

Don't ever allow yourself to be an "excusiologist." Instead, be a problem-solver.

211

People know that when they bring a problem to me, I'm going to help them solve their problem or at least help them discover a way to solve it on their own. You see, I'm convinced that *there is no problem without a solution* — and that solution is never for us to "bite the bullet" and accept defeat or loss.

Remember, you are never meant to be the loser in any situation, for God has called you to success. Look again at God's promise in Second Corinthians 2:14:

Now thanks be to God who ALWAYS leads us in triumph in Christ, and through us diffuses the fragrance of His knowledge in every place.

However, this divine promise only comes to pass in your business as you apply this next principle to your life:

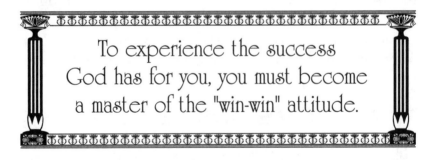

To experience the success God has for you, you must become a master of the "win-win" attitude.

If you are a Christian business person, you should strive to make sure that both sides of every transaction come out as winners. The consumer should never feel as if he was swindled or cheated. Instead, he should walk away happy, feeling like he got the greatest deal on the face of the earth. At the

212

same time, you should be happy with the outcome of each transaction as well.

Don't let yourself live your life the way much of today's world does: by means of excuses. Don't start complaining, "If only this would have happened, things would have been different in my life." Going through each day as an excusiologist not only results in unfulfilled dreams, but also in a depressed attitude toward life.

One common situation I've seen in dealing with Christian business people is this: Discouraged by failure, they live their lives by excuses as they wait for the Holy Spirit to come down and change their business for the better in one fell swoop.

Friend, the Holy Spirit is not going to change your business in one fell swoop. He may change *you* in one fell swoop, but that isn't the way He's going to change your business!

You must realize that life in every way, shape, and form is a result of *attitude*. Life is a series of *choices*, not a series of *chances*. Therefore, the following principle is a key to your success in business and in life in general:

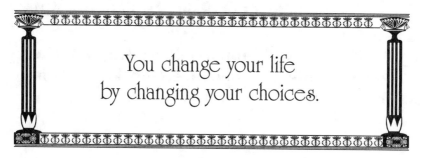

You change your life
by changing your choices.

213

By changing your outlook on life, you can change anything about yourself that needs to be changed. The way you think about yourself is a crucial key in attaining excellence in the workplace. One of the greatest truths ever written by Solomon, found in Proverbs 23:7, says, **"For as he thinks in his heart, so is he...."**

Other people may see you as a success, but how do you see yourself? You will never obtain success in your business until you think you are a success.

Do you realize that most people succeed out of fear of failure? Most people are so afraid of poverty that it drives them to achieve. They'll work their fingers to the bone, saving every penny they can and never enjoying the fruits of their labor along the way. Others have learned how to enjoy life without ever learning how to pay for it.

We can find God's balance in Ecclesiastes 5:19,20:

> **As for every man to whom God has given riches and wealth, and given him power to eat of it, to receive his heritage and rejoice in his labor — this is the gift of God.**
>
> **For he will not dwell unduly on the days of his life, because God keeps him busy with the joy of his heart.**

May God help us strike the proper balance as we learn to change our attitudes according to His Word!

Move in God's Timing

I want to share some specific principles with you that will help you change your experience in the business realm as they help you change your attitudes. Here's the first one:

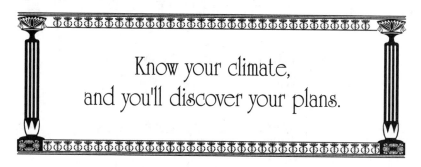

Know your climate, and you'll discover your plans.

In other words, don't try to sell steaming hot coffee on a 98-degree day!

You must understand the financial climate, the business climate, and the consumer climate in which you live. Let me give you an example. For a number of years, people wrote letters or talked to me about expanding the scope and outreach of this ministry to a national level through television and other means. But although I received all this outside counsel, I determined to wait on God's timing. I understood the importance of this principle:

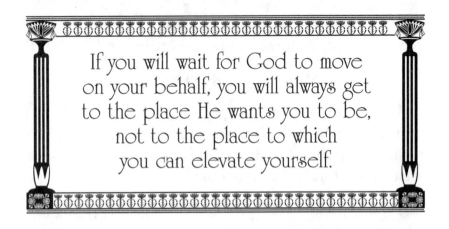

If you will wait for God to move on your behalf, you will always get to the place He wants you to be, not to the place to which you can elevate yourself.

This leads to another principle that will help you understand your own personal "climate":

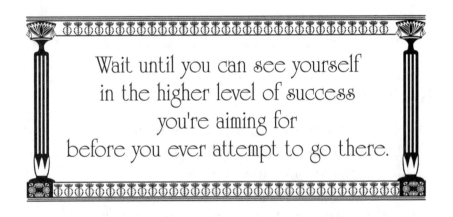

Wait until you can see yourself in the higher level of success you're aiming for before you ever attempt to go there.

That's the way I approached the issue of expanding the ministry several years ago. For an entire year, I shut everything down and didn't expand because I was unsure about myself. I was unsure about who I was, where I was, and whether or not I had enough inner maturity and strength to successfully go on to the next level of ministry that I believed God was placing before me.

We always have to make sure we have enough of what it takes to achieve success at the next level. In Luke 14:28-32, Jesus gives us this principle in two different parables:

"For which of you, intending to build a tower, does not sit down first and count the cost, whether he has enough to finish it--

"lest, after he has laid the foundation, and is not able to finish, all who see it begin to mock him,

"saying, 'This man began to build and was not able to finish.'

"Or what king, going to make war against another king, does not sit down first and consider whether he is able with ten thousand to meet him who comes against him with twenty thousand?

"Or else, while the other is still a great way off, he sends a delegation and asks conditions of peace.

Many business people launch out in such a way that they leave no possibility for retreat in case they encounter the need to back up and make adjustments. They begin their venture without understanding what it will cost to maintain the new level they're heading for. As a result, they embarrass themselves when they get halfway out and find they can neither go forward nor make the return trip. They can't finish the work they've started because the cost became greater than they anticipated.

That situation may sound all too familiar to you. If so, I have some good advice for you:

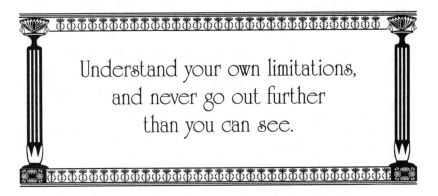

Understand your own limitations, and never go out further than you can see.

You may be tempted to go further than what you can see at the present time. You may think, *If I just go a little bit further, the return is going to be better.* No, it isn't. Take your time. Understand the climate in which you live. Understand your own limitations and abilities. There is nothing wrong with taking just a half step at a time. Don't try to hit a grand slam every time you get up to the plate!

This is one principle I understand well. Sometimes I move so slowly that many might think I'm doing nothing. But understand this: I never go backwards. I never have to retreat because I only move forward when I know I'm ready and the timing is right.

So take your time as you strive to build your business. Slow down. Instead of always waiting for God to work a miracle by causing that big deal to come through, take a small step yourself; then put your stake in the ground. Then take another small step, and once more put your stake in the ground. It may seem that this method is taking too much time, but I promise you that it is a much more effective way to successfully reach your goal!

I remember the time a principal of a Christian school told me about a great miracle God had done for her. It was Friday, and the school didn't have enough funds to make payroll. So the principal went out behind the school building and prayed, "God, You have to come through for us! I need $2,200 to pay these teachers within an hour, or we're going to have to shut down the school!" (That may not seem like a large amount to you, but $2,200 seems like $1,000,000 to the person who doesn't have it.)

Suddenly a car came around to the back of the building where the principal was praying. The principal didn't even know the person in the car; nevertheless, he drove over to her, handed her a paper sack, and then sped off. The principal looked in the sack. There was a pile of $100 bills in there — twenty-two in all!

This woman really wanted me to get excited about her testimony, but all I could say at the time was "That's interesting." Later I went before the Lord and said, "Okay, Lord, You need to help me understand something here. Why haven't You ever come behind *my* building and given *me* $2,200 when I needed it? You've never worked a miracle like that in the financial realm for me!"

But the Holy Spirit immediately stopped me and spoke to my heart: "Would you like to need a miracle in the financial realm?"

"No, Sir," I answered.

"Then what are you complaining about?" He asked.

The Holy Spirit had a good point there! I may seem slow, but I've always had the money to move forward before I have ever launched out into a new level in ministry. For instance, when we expanded into television and started a program on TBN, we could have paid a year in advance in cash!

So don't go out further than you can see. Take your time. Then you can build your business with success instead of living on the edge all the time. God didn't call you to live on the edge as a Christian business person. He called you to *build* as you live in prosperity and abundant blessing. If you're living on the edge all the time, that means you're investing everything you have to take the next step — and if it doesn't work, you're going to fail. That isn't God's way of doing things.

Now, I realize that many Bible teachers will teach you that walking in faith means "going for broke" all the time. But most people who go for broke do just that — they go broke! I'd estimate that forty people have failed for every one person who has succeeded at this extreme method of pursuing prosperity in their business.

So what difference does it make whether you build slowly or build quickly?

Well, in my case, building slowly has enabled me to fulfill a commitment I made years ago that all the people who ever work for me would never live impoverished. I make sure my employees earn more money working for me than they can earn anywhere else. They don't have to go home and think about taking on a part-time job or getting into a multi-level company because I'm paying them what their job is worth in the marketplace. Why am I able to do this? Because I have taken my time in expanding this ministry, going no further than I could see at each level of growth.

So let's review what I've said so far about building your business successfully:

- Don't get in a hurry. Let God determine the timing for expansion and growth.

- Understand what your limitations are, but see yourself as a success.

- Don't try to go beyond the way you view yourself at any given time.

- When you can see yourself successfully maintaining a higher level, move on up to it.

Enjoy Yourself Along the Way

Here's an important principle to remember, no matter what level you're at right now as you build your business:

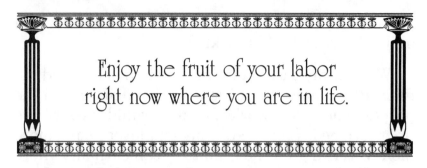

Enjoy the fruit of your labor right now where you are in life.

We already looked at Ecclesiastes 5:19 (*NIV*), which says, **"Moreover, when God gives any man wealth and possessions, and enables him to enjoy them, to accept his lot and be happy in his work — this is a gift of God."**

The Bible says that God **"...gives us richly all things to enjoy"** (1 Tim. 6:17). Yet how many people do you know who work for retirement, never enjoying themselves along the way? Finally, the day comes when they retire — but sixty days later, they die from the stress of overworking all their lives!

Enjoy every moment of every day, no matter what season of life you're in right now. If all you can afford is hamburgers, then buy yourself the best-looking hamburger you can find. Then sit down to eat with the nicest people you can find and enjoy that hamburger, thanking God for His blessings all the while!

Then as you move up to steak and on to filet mignon, keep savoring every second of your life. Enjoy the labor of your hands. Don't always be looking so far into the future that you view your present with disdain. Don't hate where you are right

222

now just because you know where you're going in the future.

Enjoy where you are at the present moment — but make sure you don't set up camp there! You have to be ready when God tells you it's time to move on.

Focus on Becoming the Best

In order to enjoy every moment of your life, it's important to find out what you really want to achieve in life. Once you know you're doing what you want to do for a vocation, this next principle will help you achieve excellence as a business person:

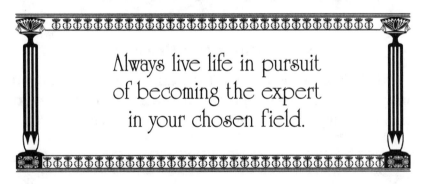

Always live life in pursuit of becoming the expert in your chosen field.

Be single-minded in pursuing the field of business you have chosen. Work on becoming the best at what you do. Don't just work with the attitude "Hey, this will make me some money. It's a living." No, go for every bit of success you can go for, but remember to enjoy yourself along the way. And don't forget to focus on God as you pursue success in your field. As you do, He will show you the wisest course to take at every turn.

Remember, in Deuteronomy 8:18, the Bible tells us that it is God who gives you the power and ability to obtain wealth:

And you shall remember the Lord your God, for it is He who gives you power to get wealth, that He may establish His covenant which He swore to your fathers, as it is this day.

If God gives you the power to obtain wealth, that means He also gives you the *ideas* and the *creativity* needed to obtain wealth. So as you seek to build your business, focus on God and His Word, trust in the Holy Spirit to guide you, and *never settle for anything less than the best*!

What About the Present?

If you're someone who dreams big dreams, you may need to pay special attention to this next principle for making your business a success:

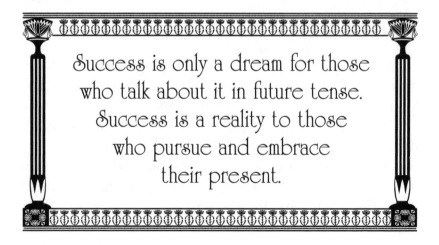

Success is only a dream for those who talk about it in future tense. Success is a reality to those who pursue and embrace their present.

Many people talk about the great things they're going to achieve when they get old. But what are they doing right now to plan and prepare for their future?

Certainly every one of us needs to have a vision to fulfill, a goal to pursue, a dream to achieve. But a dream is no good if we just talk about it and never do anything about it.

The reason I can say this to you is that I have been guilty of this very thing in the past. At times I've talked and talked and talked about certain dreams I wanted to see fulfilled, but then I never did anything about those particular dreams.

With every dream you talk about, there comes a time when you just need to take action on what you have said you believe. As you put your plan into action in the present, you are laying the foundation for your dream to be fulfilled in the future.

Be Enthusiastic!

This next principle is so important for Christian business people to get ahold of.

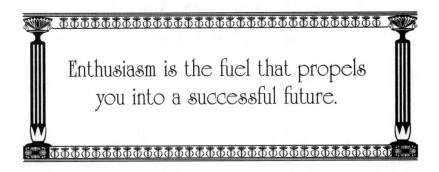

Enthusiasm is the fuel that propels you into a successful future.

Get excited about what you do in your business! Be excited about all the things God wants to do through you. Your enthusiasm displays your outlook on life.

I have a friend who has a plaque with a motto hanging on the wall behind his desk. It says this: "Get enthusiastic within ten seconds, or get out of here." You know, that is absolutely true. You should get excited about what you're doing or get out of it. I'm not talking to you as a person who wants to make a living; I'm talking to you as one who wants to change a generation.

Do you want to change your generation, or do you just want to make money? Making money is easy. I can't understand why people have such a hard time doing it. The challenge is in changing a generation. But remember, a challenge always offers the reward of gold to bring back home. There are always spoils to a war.

So go out and conquer, becoming the best you can be in the business world. Meanwhile, stay enthusiastic not only about excelling in your work, but about changing your generation!

Stay Honest With Yourself

Here's another principle I think you'll relate to:

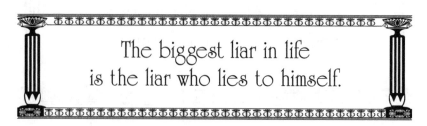

The biggest liar in life
is the liar who lies to himself.

Many times Christian business people lie to themselves about how far they have progressed toward their dreams. They also tend to lie to themselves about the current status of their business. Eventually they lie, not only to themselves, but to other people about what is going on in their lives and their business.

Don't lie to yourself about how you are doing spiritually and in the running of your business. This applies in a positive context as much as it does in a negative context. When God is blessing your business and working out great things in your life, don't stand there and say He isn't. But also, don't lie to yourself by saying everything is going great when you know there are things that need adjustment in your life and business.

Integrity Without Exception

I put a great amount of stress on these next two principles:

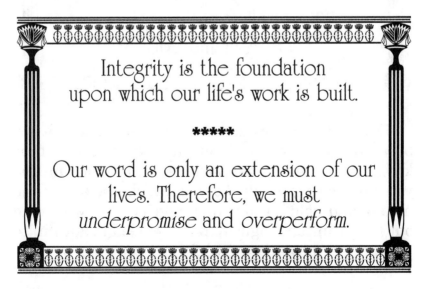

Integrity is the foundation upon which our life's work is built.

*****

Our word is only an extension of our lives. Therefore, we must *underpromise* and *overperform*.

227

It is so important to conduct yourself as a person of integrity, no matter what problem or challenge you may be facing in your business dealings. Regardless of the circumstances, your goal should always be to *underpromise* and *overperform.*

To be people of excellence in the business world, we must demonstrate that we will keep our word, no matter what. We are to be absolutely committed to keeping the Word of God and to keeping our own word.

I determined long ago that I would never knowingly break my word. After all, I have to go home with Jesus every night! That's what you have to do as well to be a person of excellence in the business world.

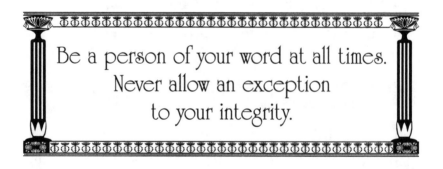

Be a person of your word at all times. Never allow an exception to your integrity.

Don't ever allow an exception in your life for breaking your word. Even if you find out that keeping your word on a business transaction means you will lose a great deal of money, choose to lose the money and hold on to your integrity. You will come out better in the long run, because God is faithful to reward you as you are faithful to keep your word.

This is admittedly a high standard to live by, but it is the level of honesty God expects of you as a person of excellence. You are never to allow a lapse in your integrity. Thus, your reputation for honesty and integrity will allow both the people you work with and the people you serve to put their trust in you. Perhaps now you can see why the prerequisite for God prospering your business is that you are true to yourself as well as truthful to others.

The Power of Association

This next principle highlights the importance of your everyday decisions in determining the outcome of your business and, indeed, your life:

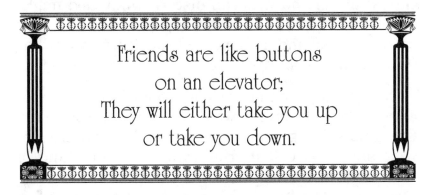

Friends are like buttons on an elevator; They will either take you up or take you down.

What kind of people do you associate with? Are they successful in their chosen field? Are they people who strive for excellence?

Take the time to answer that question honestly. Find out if you want to be like those with whom you associate closely. If you're not hanging around people you want to be like, you better change your company!

Remember, the Bible says, **"He who walks with wise men will be wise, but the companion of fools will be destroyed"** (Prov. 13:20).

Of course, you should always be ministering to people as you go through each day. But you should have a different relationship with the people you minister to than you have with those who are closest to you.

I don't allow the people to whom I minister into my personal life. I never tell them any of my secret dreams. Why not? Because Joseph told his dreams to the wrong people, and he ended up in jail! That's why I only share my dreams with those who are closest to me and who can discern what God might be saying to me. These are the people who can best encourage me and help me find the doorway to what God has for me in life.

I have high standards for whom I allow to get close to me because I want to be wise. Too many Christians hang around with people who are not wise and then call it friendship. But that kind of friendship doesn't fit the Bible's definition found in Proverbs 27:6: **"Faithful are the wounds of a friend, but the kisses of an enemy are deceitful."**

Most people look for others who will accept them in their folly. They associate friendship with *comfort*. But according to this verse of Scripture, friendship and comfort are not the same.

True friendship means I can trust someone enough to let him pull the splinter out of my eye, knowing that, in the process, he won't hit me with a two-by-four that's stuck in his own eye! In other words, I know my friend won't point his finger at me in an effort to cover his own sin.

My friend is also the kind of person who tolerates nothing but excellence in every area of life. This is the kind of person I want to try to be like; therefore, this is the kind of friend I allow to walk alongside me through life.

Be Willing To Do The 'Dirty Work'

As your business grows, you may become tempted to give to someone else the responsibilities you don't like to deal with. That's why I believe it's important to stress this principle to you:

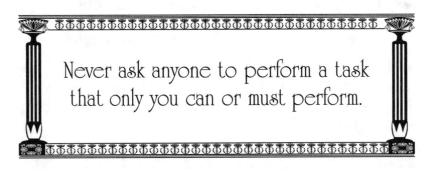

Never ask anyone to perform a task that only you can or must perform.

Don't pass off your dirty work to your subordinates. Don't delegate the responsibilities that are rightfully yours to fulfill.

One of my staff members recently said to me, "I know you have a lot going on in your responsibilities with the church and ministry. Is there anything I can do to take some of that load off your shoulders?"

"Honestly," I said, "there really isn't anything you can do. Every one of the things I am facing, I must face alone."

I will not relinquish my responsibilities. They're mine and mine alone. I'm not going to put those responsibilities off on someone else so that, just in case the outcome isn't good, I can blame that person instead of myself.

Now, that doesn't mean you're supposed to do everything by yourself. Certainly there are certain tasks you can delegate to others. As a business person, you need to be a good delegater with those people whom God has called to work for you. But there will always be responsibilities you cannot delegate to others because they involve matters your staff shouldn't even know about. These are the responsibilities that only you should handle.

Get Rid of Every Negative Thought

The next principle is a basic truth that will not only help you build your business successfully; it will also cause you to move toward success in every area of your life:

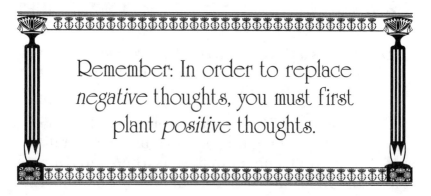

Remember: In order to replace *negative* thoughts, you must first plant *positive* thoughts.

232

Replace any thought from the devil about your business with what God says. The Bible doesn't tell you, "Thanks be unto God, who often causes you to triumph, although in your professional life you will sometimes lose." It says, **"...Thanks be to God who ALWAYS leads us in triumph in Christ..."** (2 Cor. 2:14).

Every aspect of your business will begin to line up with God's Word as you replace the devil's thoughts with what God has to say about it. It doesn't matter how long it takes. It doesn't matter what it looks like on the way. Every bit of it will line up with the Word if you will just hang in there. Stay true to your integrity. Stay true to your principles. Stay true to your word. Never allow any form of compromise to infiltrate your life at the workplace, and you will begin to see God's Word fulfilled in that area of your life.

Control Your Emotions

Besides replacing the devil's negative thoughts with God's thoughts in your mind, you must also follow this next principle:

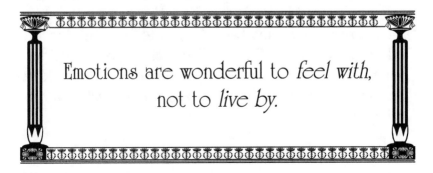

Emotions are wonderful to *feel with*, not to *live by*.

If you're not careful, your mind and emotions will run wild on you when you face difficult challenges in your business. That's why you must control your emotions and refuse to allow your passions to control *you*. Keep your emotions under lock and key as you continue to do the right thing, day after day after day.

Very few people know how to live by principle instead of by their emotions. In fact, in today's society, people are being taught how to fail. It's acceptable today to be dependent on someone else in order to have one's daily bread. But this faulty perspective is like a house of cards — eventually it is going to fall. When it does, it will be the believers who have been taught to think right, to control their emotions, and to live by God's principles who will pick up the pieces and move on to success.

Remember, responsibility is personal. You have a personal responsibility to grow, to win, to succeed. Therefore, whether or not you succeed in business is a matter between you and God and not anyone else.

No man can determine your success or make you successful. As Abraham said to the king of Sodom, "Let no man say that he ever made Abram rich but God alone" (Gen. 14:22,23). So on the way to building your business into a successful venture, always keep this thought in mind: *Your success is between you and God and no one else.*

Count the Cost

There is no way to get around it — to begin any new business venture requires a great deal of sacrifice and personal cost. Therefore, this next principle is a prerequisite for success before you ever take that first step of starting a new business:

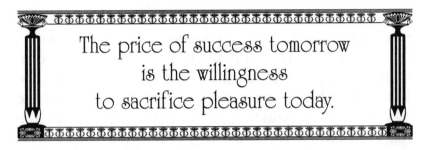

The price of success tomorrow is the willingness to sacrifice pleasure today.

I know many business people whom I consider to be very successful in what they do. I know others who are only moderately successful. Then there are those whom I call "wanna-be's" — those who want to be successful but are not. Sometimes it seems that "wanna-be's" talk more about success than the very successful do!

Let me tell you what usually happens between the stages of "wanna be" and "very successful" that keeps the number of those who actually reach the latter stage extremely low. It can all be encompassed in one small, four-letter word: *pain.*

It takes pain to succeed, so it's important to ask yourself, *Am I willing to pay the price?* Jesus said it well in Luke 14:28:

235

"For which of you, intending to build a tower, does not sit down first and count the cost, whether he has enough to finish it."

Count the cost of your business venture — and the cost of it is pain.

Believe me, friend, you'll experience rejection. You'll have people talk about you. The whole world will say you're crazy for thinking you can succeed in such-and-such a business when no one has ever done it before. But if you have a mandate from God to take that step, you'll have to endure the rejection and criticism in order to obey Him. You just have to remember this:

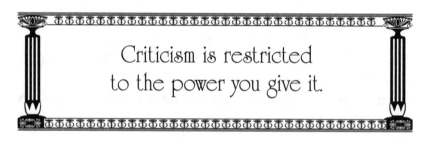

Criticism is restricted to the power you give it.

You may as well know now that success will make some people critical of you. When you're a failure at what you're doing, no one is critical of you. In fact, people like you. You're the "good ol' boy who is down on his luck like the rest of us." But when you begin to succeed, no one wants you except those who need your services or who understand success.

236

So just remember — criticism only has the power you give it in your life. Don't allow it to have any power within you.

You must also count the cost of financial sacrifice as you put together the necessary capital to make the business work. Believe me, that can be painful along the way to success. And if someone ever decides they don't want to pay you for a multiple-thousand-dollar job you did for them, that is very painful!

Nevertheless, *you don't quit.* You stay *persistent* and *consistent.* You realize that Christians who are considered failures didn't actually fail; they just quit trying. But you counted the cost before you ever took this step, and you're not a quitter. You are a success, not based on how much money you can produce, but based on what God has said about you — that you always triumph in Christ in every situation! Success may as well be your middle name because that's what God calls you!

Think of yourself as a spiritual gold miner as you press through the pain and the sacrifice of building your business. It may seem like you have to sift through the empty ore forever until you hit the vein of gold you've been looking for. But hold on to your determination not to quit. Just keep pressing through the low-level persecutions and pressures of life until you hit Holy Spirit pay dirt!

Success truly is the result of your willingness to bear pain. It is painful to live through years of building your business in which you just break even or have a very small percentage of profit. But years of prosperity and abundant blessing are coming if you will always remember that the principles that *make* you successful are the very same principles that will *keep* you successful. You cannot relinquish any of these truths once you attain your goals of success in business — for whatever you give up, you will lose.

Employer-Employee Relationships

Now I want to address the issue of employer-employee relationships. How you treat your employees is a key to building and maintaining a successful Christian business.

James 5 talks about rich men — for which we can substitute the term "employers" — who misuse their laborers:

Come now, you rich, weep and howl for your miseries that are coming upon you!

Your riches are corrupted, and your garments are moth-eaten.

Your gold and silver are corroded, and their corrosion will be a witness against you and will eat your flesh like fire. You have heaped up treasure in the last days.

Indeed the wages of the laborers who mowed your fields, which you kept back by fraud, cry out; and the cries of the reapers have reached the ears of the Lord of Sabaoth.

You have lived on the earth in pleasure and luxury; you have fattened your hearts as in a day of slaughter.

James 5:1-5

How does this passage of Scripture apply to you as a Christian employer? Well, you need to understand that God uses people in your life to help you multiply who you are and what you do. This includes your employees, whom He has called to help you multiply your business.

Because your employees have such an important role in the attaining of your business goals, these people are worthy of their pay. Colossians 4:1 expresses this principle well:

Masters, give your bondservants what is just and fair, knowing that you also have a Master in heaven.

This verse provides a vital principle for the Christian business person:

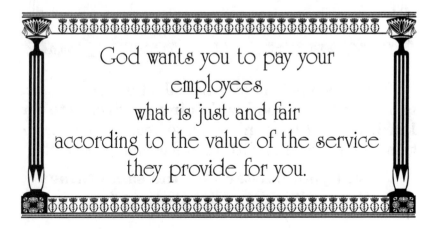

God wants you to pay your employees
what is just and fair
according to the value of the service
they provide for you.

239

As I said earlier, I endeavor to pay my employees more than what their job is worth in the marketplace. For instance, suppose a cashier came to work for me who could earn no more than $6.50 an hour working for any other company. I would pay her at least $7.00 an hour. That way I am not only paying her a fair wage, but I am blessing her beyond what her work is worth in the marketplace.

I believe a faithful employee is worth every penny you pay him because you wouldn't be able to fulfill what you are called to do without his help. Therefore, it would be better to *overpay* your employees rather than underpay them. That doesn't mean you should allow the payroll to eat dangerously into your overall profits. But your employees need to be paid well for their work in helping you multiply your business.

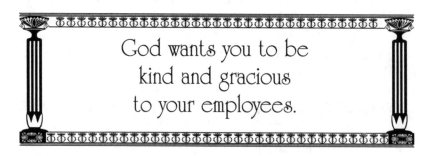

God wants you to be kind and gracious to your employees.

In Ephesians 6, it says this: Just as servants are to be busy **"with good will doing service, as to the Lord, and not to men"** (v. 7), so, too, are masters to treat their servants with kindness and good will:

And you, masters, do the same things to them, giving up threatening, knowing

that your own Master also is in heaven, and there is no partiality with Him.

Ephesians 6:9

It is important to speak kindly to your employees as you give them their instructions. Don't resort to yelling and threats if things aren't done the way you like. Remember, you are to reflect the nature of your own Master in Heaven even as you correct a situation.

Let me give you another suggestion for showing kindness to your employees in a tangible way: Every so often, make out two checks for each employee on the regular payday: one for their regular wages and one just to bless them.

You see, the nature of your relationship with your employees will make or break your business in many ways. When your employees are happy, your customers will be happy. And when your customers are happy, you are happy because your business is beginning to prosper and grow!

So get your working relationships right according to the Word of God. Be careful whom you associate with. Don't break your word. Be true to yourself. Stay focused. And always keep in mind that *your attitudes will determine your altitude*. As you follow all these basic guidelines we've talked about, you will find yourself building toward success not only in your business, but in every area of life!

PRINCIPLE FOR DEVELOPING A SOUND BUSINESS ATTITUDE

* You must develop a heart of servanthood and problem-solving for your customer base.

* It is your service to others that will manifest the by-product of personal wealth you want to obtain.

* Your attitudes in business should be reflective of your desire to serve others.

* Don't ever allow yourself to be an "excusiologist." Instead, be a problem-solver.

* To experience the success God has for you, you must become a master of the "win-win" attitude.

* You change your life by changing your choices.

* Know your climate, and you'll discover your plans.

* If you will wait for God to move on your behalf, you will always get to the place He wants you to be, not to the place to which you can elevate yourself.

* Wait until you can see yourself in the higher level of success you're aiming for before you ever attempt to go there.

* Understand your own limitations, and never go out further than you can see.

* Enjoy the fruit of your labor right now where you are in life.

* Always live life in pursuit of becoming the expert in your chosen field.

* Success is only a dream for those who talk about it in future tense. Success is a reality to those who pursue and embrace their present.

* Enthusiasm is the fuel that propels you into a successful future.

* The biggest liar in life is the liar who lies to himself.

* Integrity is the foundation upon which our life's work is built.

* Our word is only an extension of our lives. Therefore, we must underpromise and over-perform.

* Be a person of your word at all times. Never allow an exception to your integrity.

* Friends are like buttons on an elevator; They will either take you up or take you down.

★ Never ask anyone to perform a task that only you can or must perform.

★ Remember: In order to replace *negative* thoughts, you must first plant *positive* thoughts.

★ Emotions are wonderful to *feel with*, not to *live by*.

★ The price of success tomorrow is the willingness to sacrifice pleasure today.

★ Criticism is restricted to the power you give it.

★ God wants you to pay your employees what is just and fair according to the value of the service they provide for you.

★ God wants you to be kind and gracious to your employees.

NOTES:

_____

_____

_____

_____

_____

_____

_____

NOTES:

NOTES:

CHAPTER SIX

FULFILLING GOD'S WILL IN THE WORKPLACE

So many Christians are seeking to know God's will for various areas of their lives — their careers, their marriages, their children, etc. What these Christians don't realize is that it is a lot easier than they think to understand God's will. While they are scurrying around trying to discover God's unknown will about a certain area, He is trying to tell them, "Just concentrate on fulfilling My known will first, and you'll do just fine!"

So here's the final question we're going to discuss: *What is God's will for the workplace?* We'll never be able to fulfill the will of God at our jobs if we don't understand what His Word says about the subject.

You know, people in the world have a million reasons for why they pursue a career or go to work every day. They want to go to work:

- So they can become somebody in life.

- So they can gain status in the eyes of others.

- So they can boast of their lifetime accomplishments.

- So they can buy a new house, a new car, a new boat, etc.

- So they can put their children through private school.

- So they can enjoy a higher standard of living.

- So they can give their children a better life than they had growing up.

- So they can plan an exciting vacation.

As a society, we have learned how to work for our time off, not for our time on the job. Ask a person about the highlights of his life, and he'll tell you about all the wonderful things he does on vacation. Very seldom will he mention any excitement he experiences during the hours he spends at his job. His whole motivation for working is to be able to enjoy his time spent away from work.

Yet even with all these reasons Americans have for going to work, the United States has gone in the space of a lifetime from being the number-one creditor nation in the world to becoming the number-one debtor nation. No nation on the face of the earth owes more people more money than Americans do.

What has caused this downward spiral? Perhaps one of the biggest reasons is that we have gotten away from understanding God's perspective about why we work.

Work To *Give*

That's something I started asking God years ago. I prayed, "God, I want to know why *You* want me to go to work — not why *I* want to go to work. I'm not so in love with my job that I just have to go to it every day in order to be happy. I mean, I can only drive so many cars and live in so many houses! So why do You want me to work, Lord?"

I found my answer in Ephesians 4:28:

Let him who stole steal no longer, but rather let him labor, working with his hands what is good, that he may have something to give him who has need.

First, notice the beginning of this verse, where it says, **"Let him who stole steal no longer...."** This isn't talking about a thief who goes around robbing people's valuables from their houses. It's talking about us stealing from our employers. How do we steal from them?

- We steal time from our employers when our bodies are at the office, but our heart is at the lake.

- We steal the value of our labor from our employers if we spend part of our time on the job being idle.

- We steal joy from our employers if we cause problems by casting doubt about him in the minds of our coworkers.

This is in essence what Paul is saying in this scripture:

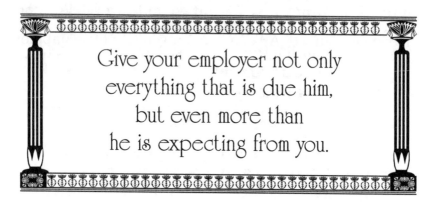

Give your employer not only
everything that is due him,
but even more than
he is expecting from you.

Now look at the rest of the verse. This is the reason God wants you to go to work:

"...working with his hands what is good, that he may have something to give him who has need."

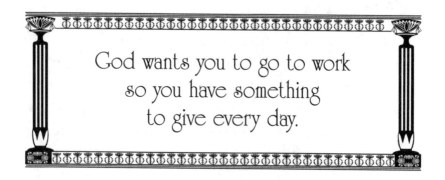

God wants you to go to work
so you have something
to give every day.

The less we go to work, the less we have to give. The less we go to work, the more we say, "Lord, bless us four and no more" and forget about the needs of everyone around us.

The more you are motivated by God's purpose for work, the more you have the needs of other people on your mind at your job rather than a new boat or a new house for yourself. All of a sudden you're a little happier as you go about your workday. You start arriving there a little earlier and leaving a little later. You stop getting involved in all the strife and stress of discontented gossip.

Now you're just happy you can help solve problems for your employer and your coworkers. You're not going to your job every day to work for yourself anymore. Your motivation has changed; you just want to give to others!

You see, God wants us to seek to be pleasing to others in the workplace. Sometimes we have a misconception about what this really means. We may think we'd demean ourselves by always seeking to please those we work for. We think, *Maybe my emotions will get all out of whack if I start trying to please my employer all the time.*

But, friend, you have to remember this:

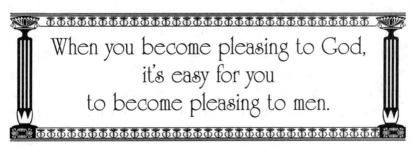

When you become pleasing to God, it's easy for you to become pleasing to men.

251

Most people make the mistake of trying to obtain the affirmation of men instead of focusing on obtaining the affirmation of God. Then they get upset when they feel slighted or passed over for a promotion.

But the situation is entirely different if you live by this principle:

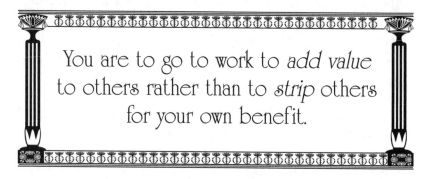

You are to go to work to *add value* to others rather than to *strip* others for your own benefit.

When your motivation is to add value, no one can ever take advantage of you. Things that once would have upset you don't even mean anything to you anymore. You're free of all that mess, because you've learned how to tap into God's will for the workplace!

Developing a Strong Work Ethic

Another aspect of fulfilling God's will in the workplace is the need to get back to that rare commodity called *a strong work ethic. The word* "ethics" refers to *a person's manners or morals.* Ethics can be said to *provide a system of principles or a set of values that teach people their duty and rule their lives in every situation, even when no one else is watching.* Ethics can also be called *a code of conduct that governs the way a person treat others.*

252

The morals and values mothers used to teach their children as a matter of course are no longer being taught on a widespread basis. Because many children are growing up without this strong ethical foundation, they don't know what is wrong or right. They grow into adulthood thinking certain sins, such as lying, cheating, and manipulating others, are acceptable. Unknown to them, their lives are on a collision course with failure, for the end of all such deception in the long term is destruction.

However, lately I've noticed that this issue of strong ethics in the workplace is becoming increasingly important. Until recently, there seemed to be a widespread acceptance of people who used others for their own advantage. But something has begun to change in our society. Employers are beginning to look for people of integrity, people who have purpose and who pursue excellence in their jobs.

Once you understand the importance of maintaining your integrity, it tends to draw out of you a desire for excellence. You want to work at a higher level of ethics than anyone else you work with has yet discovered. Why? Because you have grasped the truth of this concept:

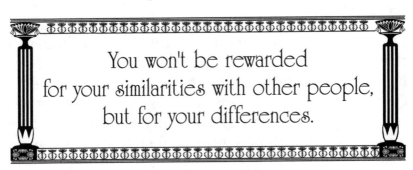

You won't be rewarded for your similarities with other people, but for your differences.

253

You know, I don't like to drive a Ford car because it reminds me of a Chevy. I don't like to eat at McDonald's because it reminds me of Burger King. No, I drive a Ford because I like a Ford. I eat at McDonald's because I like McDonald's.

In the same way, you are going to be rewarded for your differences from other people, not your similarities. So focus on those differences. In what areas do you shine? What qualities set you apart in the workplace? What causes others to gravitate in your direction rather than in another person's direction when promotion time comes around?

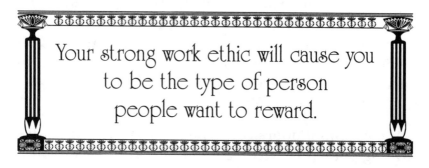

Your strong work ethic will cause you to be the type of person people want to reward.

A strong work ethic can include something as simple as being courteous to the people you work with. You see, you live in a world that has largely forsaken courtesy.

Most people are more interested in telling you how they feel about you than they are in finding out how you feel after they've blurted it all out. But a courteous person isn't just interested in spewing out his negative feelings. He actually wants to resolve any issue that causes him to feel that way, so he thinks about the consequences of his words before he speaks. Will his words cause you to feel terrible or to lose self-esteem? Will what he has to say leave you worse off than you were before?

This is just a matter of courtesy, and it is the way you need to operate in your interactions with people in the workplace. Before you try to resolve a disagreement with a coworker, consider the consequences of your words. Graciously suggest ways to fix what needs to be fixed without becoming critical and negative.

A strong work ethic also includes a constant commitment to fulfill your God-given duties on the job.

We have grown up in a generation of people who don't believe they have a duty to anyone or anything. But we each have at least one duty to mankind, and that is to make sure we're doing what God wants us to do. That duty is a part of our system of principles that we have to consider every time we are about to make a decision.

You see, if you will live your life by principles, you will never have to live it by your emotions. This brings us to an important principle to understand:

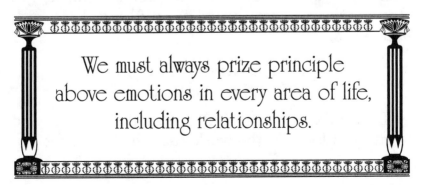

We must always prize principle above emotions in every area of life, including relationships.

If you ever catch me clicking into principle in any given situation, you'll know this: I'm sensing I can't make it in that particular situation operating in my emotions. When that happens, I switch over to my principles and, once again, I'm right on track. I'm already preprogrammed by God's holy Word to know how to respond.

For instance, when I have to correct an employee regarding something he needs to change, that employee never has to take it personally. He has just had a head-on collision with a biblical principle, not with me!

If he asks, "What did I ever do to you?" I'll just reply, "You didn't do anything to me. Psalm 51:4 says, **'Against You, You only, have I sinned, and done this evil in Your sight....'"** What he did wrong, he did against God, not me. I just have to clean up the wreck and make sure he doesn't go around justifying what he has done!"

Those types of conversations are never fun, but they are a part of my God-given duties as a pastor and an employer. My employees' job is to find out what their duties are in the workplace and then to stay continually committed to fulfilling them with excellence.

Be the Kind of Person That Sets You Apart

Let's talk further about the kind of person God wants you to be in the workplace so He can set you apart from the crowd and open doors of promotion and opportunity in your life.

1. BE AN INVITING PERSON.

Learn how to plant a magnet within your heart that draws people to you and says, "I can help you." Be approachable. Wherever you go, set an atmosphere of non-judgment in which people feel free to be themselves.

2. BE A PLEASING PERSON.

People have the idea that God doesn't want them to try to please men. But nothing could be further from the truth. Here's why:

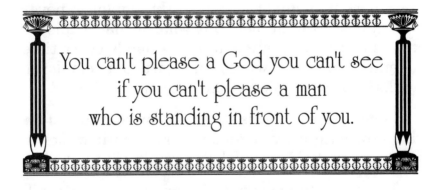

You can't please a God you can't see if you can't please a man who is standing in front of you.

People say, "I'm not a man-pleaser; I'm a *God*-pleaser!" But I don't please a man for the sake of that man. I please men because that pleases God.

The truth is, you have to be a pleaser of men in order to get anywhere in your career. Pleasing someone else besides yourself has to be your primary motive for going to work; otherwise, you won't be able to maintain a good attitude, which is so necessary for pursuing excellence at your job.

That's why you should never feel like it is wrong to want to please people. No matter how much the world makes fun of you for being a man-pleaser, keep this in mind:

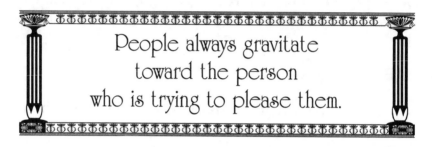

People always gravitate toward the person who is trying to please them.

A person might complain, "My employer never communicates with me!" But what if that employer knows he has an argument on his hands every time he enters the room where that particular employee works? Do you think he'll keep coming in there?

I mean, even a cow is smarter than that! If you hit that cow with a two-by-four every time it walks in the barn, that old cow will stop coming in the barn!

The same thing is true with an employer. He will gravitate toward employees who seek to please him, not toward those who always have something to complain about or who think that something is owed to them.

Therefore, you should set yourself apart in the workplace according to this principle:

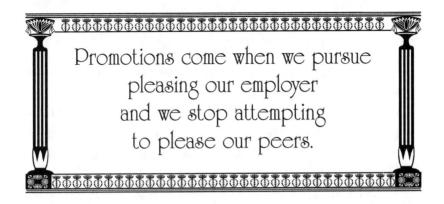

Promotions come when we pursue
pleasing our employer
and we stop attempting
to please our peers.

We spend way too much time trying to please the other people we work with instead of the person in authority over us.

You might protest, "But if I don't try to please my fellow workers, they might not like me!"

Don't let that be your greatest concern, since they may not even be in your workplace next week. Concentrate on pleasing the one to whom God has assigned you so that, when you walk in the room, he pushes through the crowd to find you!

Now, that isn't going to happen because of your great personality or creative opinions. You see, your employer isn't interested in what you think; he's interested in what *he* thinks. So pay attention to this principle:

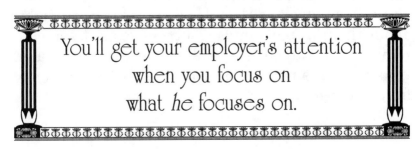

You'll get your employer's attention
when you focus on
what *he* focuses on.

259

Paul talks about this aspect of fulfilling God's will in the workplace in Ephesians 6:

Servants (slaves), be obedient to those who are your physical masters, having respect for them and eager concern to please them, in singleness of motive and with all your heart, as [service] to Christ [Himself] —

Not in the way of eyeservice [as if they were watching you] and only to please men, but as servants (slaves) of Christ, doing the will of God heartily and with your whole soul;

Rendering service readily with good-will, as to the Lord and not to men.

Ephesians 6:5-7 *AMP*

Let's look at this passage of Scripture in depth. First, we see in verse 5 (*AMP*) that, as an employee, *you are to have respect for your employer and an eager concern to please him.*

Before I go any further here, I want to remind you about this word "respect." Respect has to do with the way we treat our superiors at work. But we can't just treat our authorities respectfully with our outward actions and then dwell on negative thoughts about them in our minds. To truly respect someone requires our thoughts as well as our actions because true respect is not just an outward posture; it comes from the *heart.*

Now, let's go on to that phrase "eager concern." I like that phrase because it's a quality I want to possess in my own life. I want to eagerly pursue the pleasure of anyone in my life to whom God has assigned me. I would never want to bring displeasure to that person.

God has assigned me to certain people to help make them a success. These people are also in my life to prepare me for promotion. Therefore, I refuse to bring one second of displeasure into their lives. I won't dishonor them by falsely respecting them on the outside while secretly disrespecting them on the inside.

Here's the reason it's so important for every one of us to make that same decision in our lives:

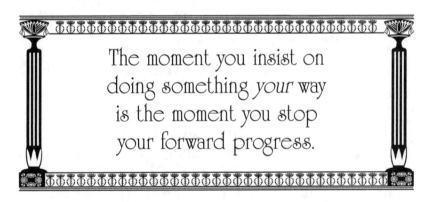

The moment you insist on doing something *your* way is the moment you stop your forward progress.

At best we will make a move laterally when we start insisting on our own way. Every time we do that, we'll run into walls in our relationships with people in the workplace. Each time we'll have to sidestep and then try again.

261

However, if we just keep trying to work things out according to what we want, we'll never do anything except move sideways. Eventually we might get what we want, but we'll never move forward into the best God has for us at our jobs.

I have an eager concern about the people to whom I submit my life. I'm concerned about knowing how to please them. I want to know both what they need and what they want. I want to know what is going to make them better people. I want to know how to cause every negative thing that ever hurt them or that was ever said about them to be erased forever.

That's the kind of attitude you need in order to please those who are over you **"...in singleness of motive and with all your heart, as [service] to Christ [Himself]"** (v. 5 *AMP*).

When you pursue pleasing your authorities with singleness of motive and with all your heart, you are really pleasing Jesus Christ Himself. You see, you won't show such eager concern to please your employer unless you are eagerly concerned about pleasing God. Your heart has to be set with a singleness of motive that can't be distracted as you pursue one primary goal while on the job — *to please the Lord.*

"Yes, but what do I do if my employer treats me wrongly?"

It doesn't matter how your superior at work treats you because your reward isn't coming from him. Your reward comes from God. Never forget:

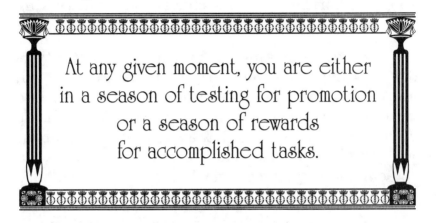

At any given moment, you are either in a season of testing for promotion or a season of rewards for accomplished tasks.

Remember, the test of a true servant is whether or not you act like a servant even when you are treated like one. If you pass that crucial test, it will be God — not your employer — who rewards you for your accomplished task.

So let's go on to verse 6 (*AMP*): **"Not in the way of eyeservice [as if they were watching you]...."** In other words, you must serve from your heart, not from your eyes. This brings up another truth you have to understand if you're going to stand out in the crowd at your workplace:

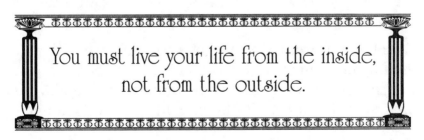

You must live your life from the inside, not from the outside.

The world has taught you that it is all right to lie and deceive other people. It's all right to live your life "in the way of eyeservice," acting one way when your authorities are watching you and talking against them when their backs are turned.

However, that kind of "eyeservice" mentality is only possible when you're trying to please a person, not God. If you want to please God, your service to your authority on the job has to come from the inside of you. You have to have the same attitudes about your employer on the inside of you that you show on the outside as you work for him day by day. That's the only way you can ever please God.

All I want to do is please God. I want God to be so happy that He wants to live with me all the time.

That's what you should want too. Don't live this life from your cranium region, giving eyeservice only to those over you in the workplace. Instead, live life from your heart. Obey the will of God with your whole heart and soul and with the singleness of one all-important motive: *to please Jesus in all you do.*

Just see what happens when you start coming to work every day feeling absolutely passionate about your job. Instead of going to work to put your time in, you'll start going there to find ways to improve your productivity.

That's a great way to get yourself in position to make more money, by the way. Just begin to be concerned about how your employer spends his business dollars. He's the one who has to somehow stretch the dollars, so he's used to being the only person who thinks about productivity. The day you start sharing his concerns is the day you set yourself apart from the crowd in his eyes!

Think about it — how many people can you think of in your workplace who are passionate about their job and eager to please their authorities? Not very many, I would imagine. That's why your employer has to hire so many employees. He could probably slash the number of his employees in half if he could just find more people who tell him, "I'm eager to serve you, and I'm here to get you a promotion!"

These are the kind of people an employer doesn't have to constantly watch to make sure they do a good job. They don't come to work in the morning carrying all the problems of their marriage and their kids. They understand this principle well:

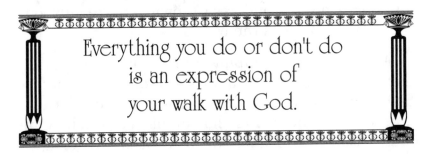

Everything you do or don't do is an expression of your walk with God.

If you mope around on the job, that is an expression of your walk with God. If you're excited about your position and the responsibilities you have to fulfill that day, that is also an expression of your walk with God.

265

Remember, you can't separate any aspect of your life from your walk with God. That's why all you do to serve your employer should be done **"...readily with goodwill, as to the Lord and not to men"** (v. 7 *AMP*).

3. BE AN OBEDIENT PERSON.

Ephesians 6:5 tells you to **"...be obedient to those who are your physical masters...."** Colossians 3:22 says it this way in the *New Living Translation:*[2]

> **You slaves must obey your earthly masters in everything you do. Try to please them all the time, not just when they are watching you. Obey them willingly because of your reverent fear of the Lord.**

Most people do the very opposite of what this verse says. Nine out of ten employees speak negatively concerning their employers at one time or another. I often wonder why people so readily bite the hand that feeds them.

Many times an employer feels like he is pulling teeth just to get his employees to do their assigned tasks. He might explain to an employee for thirty minutes why he wants that employee to follow his instructions on a particular task. But in the end, the question still comes up: "But why do I have to do it this way?"

So the employer spends another thirty minutes explaining why he as the one in charge thinks he

---

[2]*Life Application Bible: New Living Bible* (Wheaton, Illinois: Tyndale House Publishers, 1996).

made the right choice. At the end of the explanation, the employee responds, "Well, I just want you to understand the downside of what you're asking me to do." After a few versions of that scenario, that particular employee will be ripe for an industry relocation!

We are never to make our employer feel like he's pulling teeth just to get us to follow his instructions. Instead, we are to follow Paul's counsel in Colossians 3:22 and Ephesians 6:5, being obedient to our authorities at the job in everything we do.

Notice that Paul never says, "Be obedient if you want to be obedient." Yet people have inserted that kind of attitude throughout the modern workplace. That's why we have to have unions now — because we want to protect the guy who doesn't do his job. Why do I say that? Because if a person is a good worker, employers will come looking for him. I guarantee you, that person will be in great demand!

If you're an obedient employee who strives for excellence, your coworkers might say, "Hey, man, you're making us look bad!" But the truth is, they're looking bad without your help!

So never stop being obedient to your employer. No matter what anyone else says or does, just keep doing your best to please him. Meanwhile, maintain the attitude, "I want to move on up to the next level. No matter where I am in life, it's only temporary. God has another level, another promotion for me — and I'm going to attain it!"

4. BE A PERSON WITH PURE MOTIVES.

Ephesians 6:5 shows us the attitude we are to carry into the workplace every day — a determination to be obedient, respectful, and eager to please. But verse 6 also says we are to maintain that attitude not for an ulterior motive, but from a pure heart: **"...doing the will of God from the heart."**

Nothing will set you apart in the workplace more than living from a pure heart. If your supervisor asks you, "What are you here for today?" your answer should come easy: "I'm here to please you, Sir. That's my entire focus."

There's that key again: *the need to focus.* Every day you go to work, you need to focus on what you are there for. "I'm here to complete these tasks today, so this is what I will accomplish."

When your employer knows that your motives are pure and your focus is on pleasing him, he will start allowing you to make more decisions on your own. This is why:

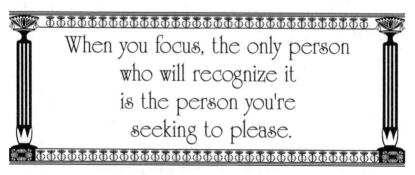

When you focus, the only person who will recognize it is the person you're seeking to please.

Every relationship in my life includes someone I am supposed to please. When I know who that person is, I focus on that person. *What can I do for him that will please him? How can I help make life easier for him?* Answering those questions is a goal I pursue from my heart because I understand this truth:

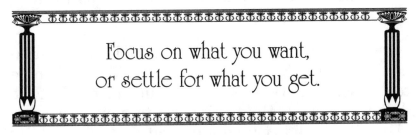

Focus on what you want, or settle for what you get.

Authority: The Way God's Kingdom Runs

Why is it so difficult even for Christians to focus on pleasing their "earthly masters"? Because they don't understand the way God's Kingdom runs. In other words, they don't understand the biblical concept of *authority.*

In Matthew 8:5-9, we read of a Roman centurion who understood how things run in God's Kingdom better than most Christians do.

Now when Jesus had entered Capernaum, a centurion came to Him, pleading with Him,

saying, "Lord, my servant is lying at home paralyzed, dreadfully tormented."

And Jesus said to him, "I will come and heal him."

The centurion answered and said, "Lord, I am not worthy that You should

269

come under my roof. But only speak a word, and my servant will be healed.

"For I also am a man under authority, having soldiers under me. And I say to this one, 'Go,' and he goes; and to another, 'Come,' and he comes; and to my servant, 'Do this,' and he does it."

Notice how this centurion described the operation of authority in his experience as a soldier. When he told a soldier, "Do this," the soldier just did it. He didn't discuss it. He didn't want to have a meeting about it. He didn't take a day off first. The soldier just did what he was told by his superior.

The centurion not only understood the way authority works in the natural realm, but he also understood that authority works the same way in God's Kingdom. Jesus marveled at this man and said to those who were willing to listen:

"...Assuredly, I say to you, I have not found such great faith, not even in Israel!
"And I say to you that many will come from east and west, and sit down with Abraham, Isaac, and Jacob in the kingdom of heaven.

Matthew 8:10,11

Jesus was saying, "The person who understands what this centurion understands is on equal par to sit down with Abraham in the Kingdom of Heaven!"

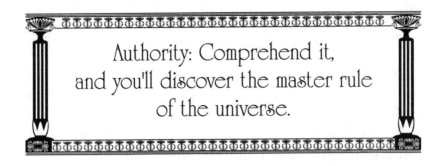

Authority: Comprehend it,
and you'll discover the master rule
of the universe.

There are people over you in life whom you are to please, and there are people under you who are called to please you. Regarding someone who understood this concept of authority, Jesus said, "I have not found such great faith among all those who say they are My followers!"

According to Jesus, then, the greatest faith of all is demonstrated by this understanding:

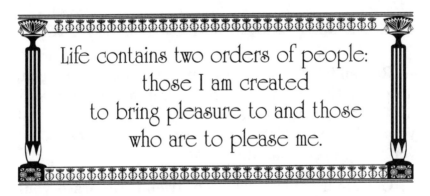

Life contains two orders of people:
those I am created
to bring pleasure to and those
who are to please me.

It's popular for people to discuss issues with their superiors. However, they often want to talk about his instructions to them with one goal in mind: to get him to change his instructions. They try to talk to him long enough to wear him out. In the end, he

271

often gives up because he is worn out from arguing, and the employees get their own way.

Yes, dialogue is very popular right now in the workplace. But there is a danger with all this dialogue. The more people talk about an issue, the more confused everything gets. As the Bible says, **"In the multitude of words sin is not lacking..."** (Prov. 10:19).

You may not agree with your supervisor's decision, but remember this principle:

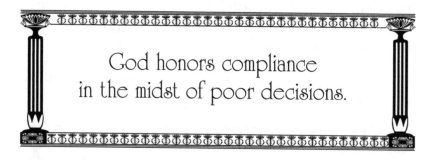

God honors compliance in the midst of poor decisions.

Remember, if you are going to achieve your goal for promotion in the workplace, you must point your life in that direction. You will never be promoted at your job if you talk to the other employees about your employer's bad decisions.

Get smart about your job, friend. Embrace your employer, not your coworkers. Coworkers who always want to question their employer aren't going to do a thing for you. But if you embrace your employer and refuse to go along with others who criticize him, you will go a long way in building your relationship with the one you are employed to help.

272

Here's the principle to remember:

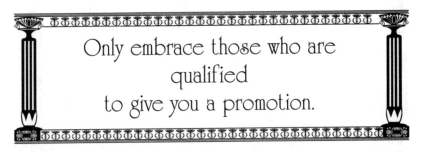

Only embrace those who are qualified to give you a promotion.

Are you criticized when you embrace upwards? Yes, you are. However, you are only criticized by the people who have stopped their forward progress.

So what is God's will in the workplace? As we've seen, He wants you to understand the way His Kingdom works within a structure of authority. Then God wants you to *eagerly* pursue pleasing the authority who is over you in the workplace. He wants a smile to come to that person's face at work every time he thinks of you.

If you've been feeling "stuck" at your job, let me give you a suggestion that can help accelerate the time it takes for you to receive a promotion: Go to your supervisor and say, "Sir [or Ma'am], I'm asking you to tell me three things I can do that will please you. How can I do better? What can I do to be more pleasing to you?" Then focus on your performance based on your supervisor's answer.

As I mentioned earlier, promotion comes much more readily when you do more than is expected of you in the workplace. So get ahold of this truth:

273

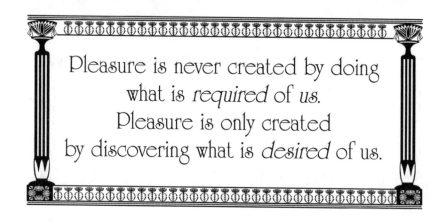

Pleasure is never created by doing what is *required* of us. Pleasure is only created by discovering what is *desired* of us.

What you do outside of your job description will bring you more than your paycheck can ever give you.

You can see why it takes much more than just desire to go to another level at your job! You have to be willing to pay the price for your employer's pleasure by going beyond your job description and by giving him your loyalty, your faithfulness, and your diligence. No matter what your employer desires for you to do, be willing to do it; then look to *God* for your promotion.

Joseph's Example of Excellence

Now let's look at one of the greatest examples of excellence ever presented in the Bible: the man called Joseph. Joseph's life demonstrated all the qualities we've discussed that lead to success, promotion, and excellence in the workplace, as well as in every other area of life.

Even with all the incredible obstacles that Joseph faced in his life, he never let those obstacles do more talking than his walk with God. No matter what was thrown at him, Joseph always stuck it through to the end. He was a person who couldn't be denied.

Joseph was the eleventh son of Jacob, the son of Jacob's beloved wife Rachel. When Joseph was only a teenager, his father gave him the coat of many colors, a coat that represented authority. This was also the time Joseph had two different dreams in which his ten older brothers bowed down in obeisance to him. Obviously, his older brothers didn't like any of this!

One day Jacob sent Joseph out to the fields to check on his ten brothers as they tended the sheep. When the brothers saw Joseph coming, they started plotting evil against him among themselves.

They said, "Here comes that dreamer — 'Daddy's pet.' He's just 'kissing up' to Daddy all the time."

Of course, anyone who "kisses up" or seeks to please his authority all the time *will* be the favorite. Do you know any successful people in life who surround themselves with "Judas" types of people who would rather betray than to "kiss up"? That's why Jacob wasn't as close to his older sons — because he knew them.

Yes, these ten older sons represented ten of the twelve tribes of Israel. Nevertheless, they were tough characters. They weren't sweet little saints who had birds land on top of their staffs as they walked down the street to the synagogue humming a hymn! That just wasn't the way it was.

So these older brothers plotted together as Joseph approached in the distance: "Here comes the dreamer. Let's kill him! Let's destroy him."

However, the oldest brother Rueben wouldn't let the other men kill Joseph, so they decided to throw him in a pit. Soon they saw Ishmaelite traders coming their way, so they sold their little brother into slavery for a profit.

Then they killed a lamb and poured its blood all over Joseph's coat of many colors so they could go back to their father and tell him that their little brother had been killed by wild animals. In his grief, Jacob said, "I'll go to my grave mourning for Joseph."

Can you imagine how wicked that set of fellows had to be? They were willing to let their father go to his grave mourning over a beloved son who was supposedly killed just to cover up for their own lack of excellence!

That same unethical behavior prevails in many workplaces today. People talk among themselves at the water cooler: "I know how to get rid of 'boss's pet.' Here's what we'll do. We'll all point the finger at him. Certainly the boss will believe all of us over the word of one person!"

So Joseph was sold out by his brothers. At that point, Joseph probably felt like the whole world was against him because his brothers really were the whole world to him. Everyone had turned his back on him. No one wanted him around.

So as he traveled the many miles to Egypt with the Ishmaelite traders, Joseph probably started thinking that the problem lay with him: *Maybe I never really should have been as obedient as I was to Dad. Maybe I should have been more like my brothers — rugged and rebellious, challenging his authority when I didn't like what he said.*

When Joseph arrived in Egypt, he was taken to the slave market and bought by a man named Potiphar, one of Pharaoh's stewards. At that point, something happened inside Joseph that set him on a course to success in the midst of amazing odds: He determined that he wasn't going to mope around in Potiphar's house, thinking about all the problems, disappointments, and betrayals he had faced up to that point. Genesis 39:2 (*KJV*) tells us the result of that decision:

And the Lord was with Joseph, and he was a prosperous man; and he was in the house of his master the Egyptian.

This verse says that soon after Joseph began to work as a slave in Potiphar's home, he had become a prosperous man. Well, wait a minute. Does that mean that Joseph in his nakedness was somehow able to hide some money to bring to Egypt? No, he was just living out this basic principle of prosperity:

Prosperity is not what lives
on the *outside* of you;
prosperity is what lives
on the *inside* of you.

From the beginning of his time in Potiphar's house, Joseph began to operate according to the principles that bring promotion into a person's life: He was willing to do whatever Potiphar asked of him — to do it right, to do it fast, and to do it with a smile.

When you get to that point with your employer, you can't be controlled anymore by negative circumstances that can occur in the workplace. Your coworkers may become tangled in disagreements and fighting with their superior on the job. But the moment you begin to submit to God, you take a step above all the mess and just keep moving upward in favor with your authority.

That's what happened with Joseph. Genesis 39:3 (*KJV*) says, **"And his master saw that the Lord was with him, and that the Lord made all that he did to prosper in his hand."** That is a profound thought. *Everything* Joseph put his hand to prospered and resulted in success.

The problem with many people is that they never put their hand to anything, so they never give God

278

something to prosper for them. Then there are all those who start projects but never finish them. That is one of the greatest frustrations an employer ever endures — employees who want to be paid a good wage yet never quite complete the tasks they have been assigned to do.

That was definitely not true with Joseph. *Joseph was a finisher.* Everything he put his hand to prospered because he had discovered a key to success that many people never tap into:

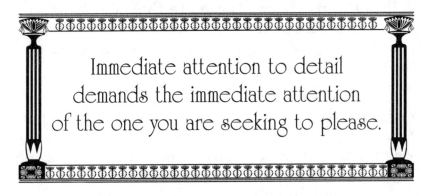

Immediate attention to detail demands the immediate attention of the one you are seeking to please.

I'll tell you, when you pay attention to the small details, you will never fail in the big things in life. The Bible says it is the little foxes that spoil the vine (Song of Sol. 2:15).

The first time an employee fails to accomplish what he has been instructed to do on a timely basis, his superior will come back and ask him, "Were you able to finish what we talked about the other day? When will it be done?" But be assured of this: A supervisor will stop seeing an employee as his "go-to" person if the same thing happens time and time again.

We must never allow the ones to whom we are responsible to look in other directions for the help they need. That is our place, not someone else's.

An employer often doesn't want to nag an employee about unfinished assignments. In that case, he only has three choices: 1) He can fire the employee for being a poor worker; 2) he can do it himself; or 3) he can look elsewhere for the one who will fulfill his vision. Those are the only choices he has. In most cases, he will not confront the employee again and again because he has to avoid taking on too many battles at one time.

So the quality about Joseph that got Potiphar's attention was not that the young man was a Jew. Egyptians hated Jews. Joseph had one God; the Egyptians had more than a thousand gods. Joseph was a dummy in this man's eyes. But there was this quality about Joseph that made him stand out from the rest of Potiphar's slaves: *No matter what Joseph was instructed to do, he did it well and in detail. Then after completing the task, he came back and asked, "Do you have other instructions for me?"*

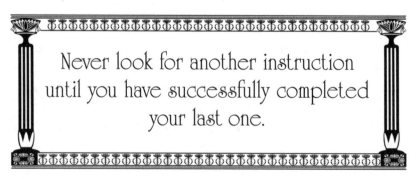

Never look for another instruction until you have successfully completed your last one.

Many times people want another instruction without finishing the last instruction they were given.

They say, "I just want to know what God wants me to do."

But what was the last thing God told them to do?

"Well, God told me to do this. But I want to hear something else from Him."

No, wait a minute. God isn't weak-minded. He isn't going to come up with a second plan for a person and say, "You didn't like My first plan? Oh, I'm sorry — here, why don't you try something else?"

No, God comes to us with something He wants done — and if we don't do it, He gives the assignment to someone else. It's the same way with our employers.

How To Find Grace In Your Employer's Sight

Now, don't get the idea that Joseph was immediately put in charge of Potiphar's household the day he was purchased as a slave. Potiphar took some time to observe Joseph's performance. The truth is, if Joseph hadn't been willing to do the menial tasks of a slave when he first came into Potiphar's house, he would never have been put in charge. He was faithful over a little before God put him in charge over much.

It's very important for you to come to this basic understanding in the workplace. The reason Joseph became a prosperous man in Potiphar's household was that *"...his master saw that the Lord was with him..."* (Gen. 39:3 *KJV*). Notice that Potiphar *saw* something. He didn't hear that Joseph was a believer. He didn't listen to Joseph witness about the Lord. Over a period of time, Potiphar *saw* that God was with Joseph and that He made all that Joseph did prosper in his hand.

Do you realize that this would never have happened if Joseph had been a bitter person? God cannot make things prosper in a person's hand when that person harbors bitterness and offense in his heart toward other people.

So consider Joseph's situation. Here was a young man who was a slave in someone's house who didn't even like him. He had been ripped away from his family and everything he loved by his own brothers. He had no promise of a future.

But for some reason, Joseph didn't spend his time moping around because of all his problems. Instead, he focused on pursuing excellence in his life and on making sure his master Potiphar was blessed. He wasn't working for his freedom. He wasn't working for a paycheck. He wasn't working for anything except for God. That's why Joseph was a study in that principle we looked at earlier: *"It is never what is done to you that determines the outcome of your life; it is how you RESPOND to what is done to you."*

What was the result of Joseph's behavior in his workplace? Verse 4 says that Joseph found grace in Potiphar's sight. Now, why do you think Joseph found grace with Potiphar? Because the Egyptian saw that God was with him.

You need to understand something, friend:

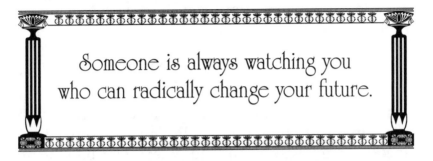

Someone is always watching you who can radically change your future.

A person might think, *As soon as God fixes this bad situation, I'm going to clean up my attitude.* No, he won't. If that person doesn't keep his attitude right in a bad situation, he won't have a good attitude when no bad situation exists. He'll find something to complain about because the root of the problem isn't in his circumstances or another person; it's in his negative response to the situation. So remember:

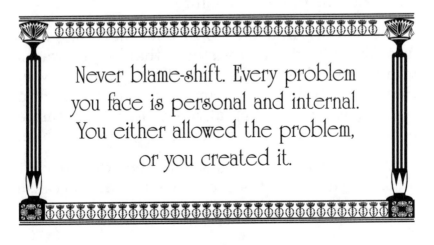

Never blame-shift. Every problem you face is personal and internal. You either allowed the problem, or you created it.

It doesn't matter who else is involved in the situation. Whatever problem comes up is yours and yours alone to deal with. The day you stop resisting this fact and start facing bad situations with a good attitude, that's the day you find grace in your employer's sight.

Get Rid of All Resistance In Your Heart

You can experience the same level of favor with your employer as Joseph did. You can come to a place in your walk with God where you become so surrendered to God's principles of excellence that your employer is unable to find a hint of resistance or rebellion in your life.

This was the quality that attracted Potiphar to Joseph. Look at what else verse 4 (*KJV*) says: **"And Joseph found grace in his sight, and HE SERVED HIM...."** Joseph served Potiphar. The Egyptian found absolutely no resistance whatsoever within this slave of his. All Joseph cared about was serving his master to the best of his ability.

It's so refreshing and so rare for an employer to find someone with no resistance that he just wants to hug you when he discovers that quality in you. However, if you serve a contrary employer from a pure heart, you can actually become his nightmare because, at that point, you actually reign above him.

Why do you think Jesus said that the greatest among God's people is the servant of all? Because the person who truly serves is the one who is in control.

You see, as long as we attempt to serve from the outside, we will be frustrated forever. *Until the day comes when we get rid of all the resistance inside our hearts, we'll live in perpetual disappointment because the actions of other people will control how we act in the workplace.*

"But my supervisor didn't include me in his planning meetings."

That's fine, God doesn't want you to be involved.

"Do you mean it doesn't bother you when you're not included in important meetings like that?"

No, it doesn't. I'll be involved when God wants me involved. Until that day, I won't be involved and I'm happy not to be. Here is why:

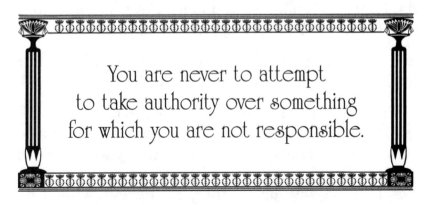

You are never to attempt to take authority over something for which you are not responsible.

I'll only take responsibility for something when I'm ready and when authority is freely given to me.

285

A person who has no resistance is a person who can be trusted because he has no agenda. An employer can be candid about the inner workings of his life because a person like that won't take advantage of him. In fact, an employee with no resistance in him may be the first person the employer has ever found who really cares about matters close to his heart as much as he cares about them.

How do you get rid of all resistance inside you? By becoming so grounded in the knowledge that God is the One who promotes you that you can say with conviction, "If I receive anything in life, it will be because God gave it to me. And if I don't receive something, it will be because God doesn't want me to have it."

That's the reason I can turn to any authority figure in my life and say, "Whatever you want me to do, I'll do it. Whatever you don't want me to have, I won't have it. You just tell me what you want."

"Yes, but what if you really want what your authority doesn't want you to have?"

It doesn't matter. If God wants me to have it, I'll get it — but I'll never rebel to get it. If God wants me to have it, I expect Him to wake up my authority in the middle of the night and give him a vision if He has to. One way or another, I'll receive what God wants me to have.

You see, I'm willing to go through present pain for future pleasure. I bow my knee now because I realize I will receive promotion from God in the future for my willing obedience.

Because Joseph lived by this principle, his authorities always promoted him. In the case of Potiphar, verse 4 (*KJV*) says, **"...he made him overseer...."** Joseph received a promotion, going straight from slave third-class to overseer, because his master had observed purity and lack of resistance within his servant's heart.

Being a true servant and a problem-solver always has to do with your heart. You begin to think more about those to whom you've been assigned than you think about yourself. You think about the problems they face every day; then you begin to solve those problems one at a time without ever having to be told to do it.

Standing Up to the Test

After becoming Potiphar's overseer, Joseph ran into a problem. You see, situations will always arise to test the purity of your servant's heart. In Joseph's case, it was a situation involving his master's wife, who wanted Joseph for herself.

The reason Potiphar's wife wanted Joseph was not just that Joseph was an attractive hunk. This woman had never met anyone like Joseph. She had never met anyone who had no resistance inside him, whose sole desire was to please.

The truth is, it's easy for a person to let down his guard around a problem-solver because he is usually very charming. However, Potiphar's wife went much too far. She made sexual advances to Joseph, thinking he would be easy to convince because he was so eager to please.

But notice Joseph's reaction:

But he refused and said to his master's wife, "Look, my master does not know what is with me in the house, and he has committed all that he has to my hand.

"THERE IS NO ONE GREATER IN THIS HOUSE THAN I, nor has he kept back anything from me but you, because you are his wife. How then can I do this great wickedness, and sin against God?"

Genesis 39:8,9

Notice that Joseph makes no bones about his high position in Potiphar's household. You see, a problem-solver can be very confident as well. Joseph was saying, "I know that there is no one greater on staff than I am. When I walk into a room, everyone else who works for the master will move out of the way because they realize the position I hold with the person they serve. It isn't that they are less than I am; it is just that I have chosen to be a problem-solver. They want someone to solve their problems — I don't. I want to solve others' problems."

You have to choose which side you're going to live your life on. But before you choose, remember this:

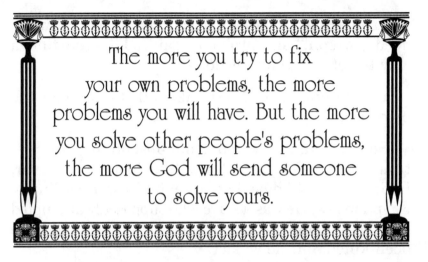

The more you try to fix your own problems, the more problems you will have. But the more you solve other people's problems, the more God will send someone to solve yours.

Notice again what Joseph said to Potiphar's wife:

"There is no one greater in this house than I, nor has he kept back anything from me but you, because you are his wife. How then can I do this great wickedness, and sin against God?"

Genesis 39:9

This woman had just run smack dab into an impenetrable obstacle by her wrong intentions. She had not run into Joseph *the problem-solver,* but Joseph *the man of principle.*

When you live your life as a problem-solver, opportunities will arise for you to do wrong. Some of those opportunities will be presented to you as shortcuts to your goals. More than likely, this is what occurred in the conversation between Potiphar's wife and Joseph. No doubt she promised him the moon if he would only comply with her wishes.

"You'll have everything you could ever want or need, Joseph," she probably said. "I'll even find a way to get you your freedom!"

But Joseph said, "No thanks. I'll stand under the pressure."

So Potiphar's wife lied about Joseph to get him in trouble, and Potiphar threw him in jail. However, Potiphar *should* have had Joseph killed according to Egyptian law. He was a slave who supposedly attempted rape on a member of the aristocracy. He should have been killed, but he wasn't.

Why wasn't Joseph killed? Because Potiphar knew that his wife was lying and that Joseph was telling the truth. He had watched the young man. He knew Joseph was a principled man. He knew Joseph would never have betrayed him. So Potiphar put Joseph in prison because he believed his slave more than he believed his wife.

Now, Joseph wasn't just put in the common people's prison. He was put in the prison where Pharaoh kept his prisoners. This was the "country club" of jails — the prison for white-collar crimes.

When Joseph arrived at the prison, his reputation had preceded him. Soon the prison warden put him in charge of the prison. Why? Because Joseph solved problems everywhere he went. Therefore, he went from running Potiphar's household to running the prison.

Consider for a moment how many times God had to rely on Joseph's character in order to bring to pass the salvation of Israel through him. Again and again God relied on Joseph's ability and willingness to overcome insurmountable odds so He could use Joseph to fulfill His plans and purposes.

Joseph had to conquer what most men never conquer — his flesh. While in Potiphar's house, he had to conquer bitterness, strife, anger, and rejection regarding what his brothers did to him. Then he went to prison and had to do it all over again regarding Potiphar's wife!

While in prison, Joseph had to solve the problems of the people he met in there for thirteen long years. In the second year of imprisonment, he solved the mystery of the cupbearer's and the baker's dreams. Yet even though his interpretations of the dreams were correct, once again Joseph was not given his just due.

As Joseph predicted, the baker was beheaded and the cupbearer was restored to his position before the Pharaoh. But for many years Joseph remained in jail as the cupbearer went about his business and forgot about him.

Nevertheless, Joseph still determined, "No, I'm not giving up because of this offense either. I will not take this into account. I'm not going to dwell on the offense in my mind. It doesn't matter; God will take care of me."

"Yes, but you should be able to get out of that prison, Joseph. You're innocent!"

"I'm not going to dwell on that," Joseph decided. "For now, I am a prisoner. I am here to run this prison. I will solve every problem I can for the prison warden. That's why I'm here. Wherever I am, I will solve the problems of those to whom I am assigned. Right now I'm assigned to the warden, so I will solve his problems."

Then Pharaoh had two mysterious dreams of his own — dreams that no one was able to interpret. Suddenly the cupbearer remembered Joseph. Joseph had remained faithful to his role as a problem-solver and servant; now the door of opportunity and promotion had finally opened to him.

Joseph not only interpreted Pharaoh's dreams for him, but he also told Pharaoh what God wanted him to do in response to the dreams. Joseph explained, "You need to find someone who is extremely smart. He needs to be able to gather 20 percent of your people's grain every year for seven years. There will be seven bumper crops, and then there will be seven years of absolute devastation. During those last seven years, the people will have the stored grain to see them through the famine."

Pharaoh thought for a moment, wondering, *Where am I going to find a man such as Joseph describes?* And then it occurred to him — he had an expert problem-solver standing right in front of him!

Meanwhile, Joseph never said a word to promote himself. You see, a problem-solver never becomes opportunistic. Joseph was willing to return to prison and continue to solve his prison warden's problems. His eyes were on God for his promotion, not on man.

But Pharaoh said, "Wait a minute. It's obvious that you have the Spirit of God in you, Joseph. I'm putting you in charge. There will be no one in all of Egypt who will be greater than you. In fact, the only thing that separates your greatness from mine is this throne!"

During the seven years of plenty, Joseph gathered together a fifth of Egypt's grain for the coming famine. Then for seven years while famine reigned, God amassed the wealth of the known world at that time and put it inside Egypt as Joseph sold that grain to everyone who came to him for help. It was the first wealth transfer ever recorded in the Scriptures. Later, after being delivered from four hundred years of Egyptian slavery, the children of Israel would walk out of Egypt with that same wealth transferred to them:

He also brought them out with silver and gold, and there was none feeble among His tribes.

Psalm 105:37

Why was such a feat possible? Because one man chose to solve problems as he waited for God to promote him to the position he had been called to fill.

What would happen in *our* lives if we made that same decision? What wonderful plans could God accomplish through us if we determined to overcome every obstacle and stay faithful to His purposes until the end? I'm telling you, the possibilities are endless because we really don't know what God has planned for our future.

It's all in our hands. Each of us can make sure that we enter into the fullness of God's will for our career, our business, or our place of employment. We just have to follow Joseph's example of excellence by developing true servant's hearts. Then we must become eager and willing problem-solvers for those to whom we are assigned.

I've given you a host of tools to use — scriptural principles that will help you pursue *God's* standard of excellence in the workplace. Now the rest is up to you. Use those tools to build a solid platform of godly character and good work habits in your life. Then launch off that platform to rise to the next level of excellence in God!

PRINCIPLES FOR FULLFILLING GOD'S WILL IN THE WORKPLACE

★ Give your employer not only everything that is due him, but even more than he is expecting from you.

★ God wants you to go to work so you have something to give every day.

★ When you become pleasing to God, it's easy for you to become pleasing to men.

★ You are to go to work to *add value* to others rather than to *strip* others for your own benefit.

★ You won't be rewarded for your similarities with other people, but for your differences.

★ Your strong work ethic will cause you to be the type of person people want to reward.

★ We must always prize principle above emotions in every area of life, including relationships.

★ You can't please a God you can't see if you can't please a man who is standing in front of you.

★ People always gravitate toward the person who is trying to please them.

★ Promotions come when we pursue pleasing our employer and we stop attempting to please our peers.

★ You'll get your employer's attention when you focus on what *he* focuses on.

★ The moment you insist on doing something *your* way is the moment you stop your forward progress.

★ At any given moment, you are either in a season of testing for promotion or a season of rewards for accomplished tasks.

★ You must live your life from the inside, not from the outside.

★ Everything you do or don't do is an expression of your walk with God.

★ When you focus, the only person who will recognize it is the person you're seeking to please.

★ Focus on what you want, or settle for what you get.

★ Authority: Comprehend it, and you'll discover the master rule of the universe.

★ Life contains two orders of people: those I am created to bring pleasure to and those who are to please me.

★ God honors compliance in the midst of poor decisions.

★ Only embrace those who are qualified to give you a promotion.

★ Pleasure is never created by doing what is *required* of us. Pleasure is only created by discovering what is *desired* of us.

★ Prosperity is not what lives on the *outside* of you; prosperity is what lives on the *inside* of you.

★ Immediate attention to detail demands the immediate attention of the one you are seeking to please.

★ Never look for another instruction until you have successfully completed your last one.

★ Someone is always watching you who can radically change your future.

★ Never blame-shift. Every problem you face is personal and internal. You either allowed the problem, or you created it.

★ You are never to attempt to take authority over something for which you are not responsible.

★ The more you try to fix your own problems, the more problems you will have. But the more you solve other people's problems, the more God will send someone to solve yours.

NOTES:

_____

_____

_____

_____

_____

_____

NOTES:

PRAYER OF CONSECRATION

Heavenly Father, I thank You that You have destined me to triumph in every situation. You have called me to personal responsibility; You have called me to excellence.

I purpose right now to pursue excellence at my job without compromise. I will exceed expectations. I will outdo all past records. I will be everything You have called me to be in my place of work.

I look to You, Father, and not to man for my promotion. Everything I do at work, I do as unto You. I will be a solver and not a creator of problems for my employer. Every problem that he brings to me today, I will solve with Your help — cheerfully, quickly, accurately, and thoroughly.

You created me to win, Father, and by Your grace I will win in every situation I face at the job today. I will not become weary in well-doing. I will not throw in my hand and stop showing respect to those God has assigned to be over me. Therefore, I know that the ultimate harvest in my workplace will surely come!

APPENDIX 1

PRINCIPLES OF EXCELLENCE ON THE JOB

APPENDIX 1
PRINCIPLES OF EXCELLENCE ON THE JOB

FOCUS:

- Focus on what you want, or settle for what you get.

- All of us have twenty-four hours each day. How we spend our twenty-four hours will determine the outcome of our lives.

- The only way to multiply your life investments and accelerate your growth is by pursuing excellence in the arenas of your intended focus.

- God has given you a position that takes 100 percent of your focus. The moment you start criticizing your employer is the moment you have moved off the post to which you have been assigned.

- You'll get your employer's attention when you focus on what he focuses on.

- When you focus, the only person who will recognize it is the person you're seeking to please.

- Satan can never schedule your *destruction*; he can only schedule your *distraction*.

- You are never rewarded for your intentions. You are only rewarded for your completions — the actions that push you toward excellence.

- In order to multiply what God has invested in you, you have to be able to *fully execute*.

- Never look for another instruction until you have successfully completed your last one.

- Refuse to move from the center of your assignment until you can say, "It is finished."

- Broken focus is the only reason for failure. Follow-through and completion is the only door to promotion.

SERVANTHOOD:

- You must become a servant before you can ever qualify yourself as a true problem-solver in the eyes of Jesus.

- The test of a true servant is if you act like a servant even if you are treated like one.

- Offense is never allowed to enter the atmosphere of a divine servant.

- A mark of a true servant is that he has abandoned all personal pressures in order to become a tool in the hand of the one he serves.

- If you don't embrace the testing grounds in life, you can never be promoted, for the testing ground in life is God's chosen place of reward.

- You are not to be faithful according to the standards you have set for yourself. Faithfulness is defined by the standards of the one God has assigned for you to serve.

- You are not to be faithful according to your standards. You can only be faithful according to the standards of the one to whom God has assigned you to serve.

- Give your employer not only everything that is due him, but even more than he is expecting from you.

- God wants you to go to work so you have something to give every day.

PROBLEM-SOLVING:

- Don't ever allow yourself to be an "excusiologist." Instead, be a problem-solver.

- Your value to your employer is in direct proportion to the problems you're willing to solve for him.

- You will only be remembered for the problems you solve or the problems you create.

- Become indispensable where you work by solving problems that other people don't want to do.

- Finances are awarded to the employee who makes solving problems his focus.

- God never designed us to solve our own problems. We were designed to solve the problems of others.

- Whatever good we do for another, God will cause to happen for us.

- The only way you can tell you are a true problem-solver is when God begins to take care of *your* problems.

- No one on earth can ever stand in the way when Heaven has decided to advance a problem-solver.

- The most effective way to deal with people who refuse to solve problems for you is to solve their problems first.

- Passionately pursue solving problems for your employer before they become your assignment.

- You are not rewarded for your value as a person. You are rewarded for the types of problems you are willing to solve for others.

- When you solve a greater problem, you will be more greatly rewarded.

- Always give the person you are seeking to please what he wants — not what *you* want him to give him.

- Don't try to compete with people; compete against mediocrity.

- Ask your boss to write down a list of every task he has asked someone to do that was left undone; then complete each of these tasks one at a time.

- You won't be rewarded for your similarities with other people, but for your differences.

- When you solve a problem, solve it cheerfully, quickly, accurately, and thoroughly.

- If you cultivate the habit of immediate attention to small details, you will never fail in the big things of life.

- Prosperity is summoned to your life the moment you give attention to detail.

- Immediate attention to detail demands the immediate attention of the one you are seeking to please.

- A problem-solver is good to all, but especially good to a few.

- Posture yourself as a "go-to" person by solving every problem to which you *are assigned*.

- Every time your superior comes to you, make him feel good about giving you something else to do.

- Follow "the law of the first" by choosing to be the first problem-solver in any relationship. Then watch as God solves your problems through others.

- The more you try to fix your own problems, the more problems you will have. But the more you solve other people's problems, the more God will solve yours.

- Leaders in every area of life will gravitate to the person who answers their most immediate need.

- Work as unto the Lord to help your supervisor get promoted.

- Problem-solving is doing more than you need to before you're asked to — not because you have to, but because you *want* to.

PROMOTION:

- If you will wait for God to move on your behalf, you will always get to the place He wants you to be, not to the place to which you can elevate yourself.

- At any given moment, you are either in a season of testing for promotion or a season of rewards for accomplished tasks.

- God alone is the One who determines your position in the vocation He has called you to fulfill.

- If you will wait for God to move on your behalf, you will always get to the place He wants you to be, not to the place to which you can elevate yourself.

- Spend an extra amount of time praying for an unfair supervisor to get a promotion.

- Someone is always watching you who can radically change your future.

- Promotion is never granted by performing the tasks you are already paid to do.

- Promotion is the reward you receive when you stand head and shoulders above others in the eyes of your authority.

- You will receive a promotion when you successfully overcome the problems you are presently paid to solve.

- To experience the success God has for you, you must become a master of the "win-win" attitude.

- Sacrifice is the road traveled by the Excellent on their journey to their divine destiny.

MOTIVATION:

- God has called you to win. He has created you to be a bearer of the One who created the universe with the words of His mouth.

- Success is only a dream for those who talk about it in future tense. Success is a reality to those who pursue and embrace their present.

- In order for you to obtain your goal, you must continually point your life in the direction of your desired destination.

- Enthusiasm is the fuel that propels you into a successful future.

- Always live life in pursuit of becoming the expert in your chosen field.

- Seeking money above the will of God will first destroy the purity of your focus — and then it will destroy you.

- You are to go to work to *add value* to others rather than to *strip* others for your own benefit.

- Enjoy the fruit of your labor right now where you are in life.

- Remember: In order to replace *negative* thoughts, you must first plant *positive* thoughts.

- The price of success tomorrow is the willingness to sacrifice pleasure today.

- There is no such thing as a shortcut to the higher levels of excellence in life.

ETHICS:

- Integrity is the foundation upon which our life's work is built.

- It is never what is done to you that determines the outcome of your life; it is how you *respond* to what is done to you.

- A person of excellence responds to God's commands with unquestioned obedience.

- Never make a decision that could possibly compromise the future God has for you.

- You must live your life from the *inside*, not from the *outside*.

- Everything you do or don't do is an expression of your walk with God.

- The excellent require God's Word to evaluate their own progress.

- Prosperity is not what lives on the outside of you; prosperity is what lives on the inside of you.

- Criticism is restricted to the power you give it.

- The biggest liar in life is the liar who lies to himself.

- Never blame-shift. Every problem you face is personal and internal. You either allowed the problem, or you created it.

- Be a person of your word at all times. Never allow an exception to your integrity.

- Friends are like buttons on an elevator. They will either take you up or take you down.

- Emotions are wonderful to *feel with*, not to *live by*.

- We must always prize principle above emotions in every area of life, including relationships.

- The harvest of my future is hidden in my choices of today.

- God has not predestined our decisions. He has predestined the *consequences* of our decisions.

- Your strong work ethic will cause you to be the type of person people want to reward.

BE PLEASING:

- When you become pleasing to God, it's easy for you to become pleasing to men.

- You can't please a God you can't see if you can't please a man who is standing in front of you.

- People always gravitate toward the person who is trying to please them.

- The moment you insist on doing something your way is the moment you stop your forward progress.

- Promotions come when we pursue pleasing our employer and we stop attempting to please our peers.

- You are not pleasing because you have done what is required of you. You are only pleasing when you go the extra mile.

- Each time you enter the workplace, you must passionately pursue what your contribution can be, never what your reward will be.

LEADERSHIP:

- You must develop a heart of servanthood and problem-solving for your customer base.

- It is your service to others that will manifest the by-product of personal wealth you want to obtain.

- Your attitudes in business should be reflective of your desire to serve others.

- Know your climate, and you'll discover your plans.

- Wait until you can see yourself in the higher level of success you're aiming for before you ever attempt to go there.

- Understand your own limitations, and never go out further than you can see.

- Never ask anyone to perform a task that only you can or must perform.

- God wants you to pay your employees what is just and fair according to the value of the service they provide for you.

- God wants you to be kind and gracious to your employees.

- When you get someone else involved in an assignment, make sure you care about his progress, answer his questions, and inspect his work.

- Understand that people can work by steps; they cannot work by abstracts.

- Never give a person an assignment without a timeline; otherwise, it may not get done.

RESPECT:

- Authority: Comprehend it, and you'll discover the master rule of the universe.

- The outcome of our lives is almost completely dependent upon our willingness to bow our knees to those whom God puts in authority over us.

- Life contains two orders of people: those I am created to bring pleasure to and those who are to please me.

- Whatever you respect moves toward you, and whatever you disrespect distances itself from you.

- You are never to attempt to take authority over something for which you are not responsible.

- A Person of Excellence assesses who and what he is in every relationship and then postures himself accordingly.

314

- A Person of Excellence never corrects upwards.

- Never allow the invitation to intimacy to be destroyed by the contempt of familiarity.

- Know the people from whom God intends for you to access information, because these are the people who help determine the outcome of your life.

- God honors compliance in the midst of poor decisions.

- Taking your employer for granted will ruin the harvest you are designed to receive from the field in which God has set you.

- Never hold an opinion about people God has called to lead you in your life.

- We must never allow ourselves the luxury of questioning anything about those in authority over us.

- We must always remember that God has called us to cover and never to expose our authority's nakedness.

- Embrace correction from your superiors as their means of drawing closer to you, not of pushing you away.

- You requalify for promotion by getting things right first with God and then with those who are in authority over you.

- In life, we must not strive for the ability to *take criticism*, but rather pursue the ability to *receive instruction*.

- Never take an instruction from a person who is unable to give you a promotion.

- Respect for your present assignment is proof that you are expecting a future harvest.

- Refuse to put up a wall between you and your superiors at work.

- Be eager to learn how to do what you have been instructed to do.

- Greatness lies not in knowing how to complete all instructions without explanation, but in being willing to admit when you don't know how to fulfill an assigned task.

- Refuse to ask a question of someone who is unqualified to give you the answer.

- Embrace oversight, but never require it.

- Always remain thankful to God and to those over you in authority.

APPENDIX 2

PRINCIPLES OF EXCELLENCE IN COMMUNICATION

APPENDIX 2
PRINCIPLES OF EXCELLENCE IN COMMUNICATION

1. In your communication with others, always have a purpose.

2. Remember that communication is always two-way — involving both transmitting and receiving.

3. Weigh your words. Never say anything you don't want to come to pass because your words are spirit and go into eternity.

4. Words paint pictures. Begin by painting a picture of your goal for the conversation.

5. The goal you want to achieve is the other person's understanding of the problem they need to solve. Set a course for that goal; then through dialogue, make your adjustments.

6. Be a good listener.
   "So then, my beloved brethren, let every man be swift to hear, slow to speak, slow to wrath" (James 1:19).

7. Show a genuine interest in what the other person is saying.

8. Invite a person to communicate with you by always making eye contact with him.

9. Always posture yourself as the receiver in every conversation.

10. Stay engaged in the conversation from beginning to end.

11. Don't drift in the conversation to another subject. Stay on track.

12. Use diplomacy, because kindness changes people's hearts.

13. Be discreet. Know when to speak and when not to speak.

14. Understand your position in every conversation, and refuse to cross boundaries.

15. Don't assume the other person understands you.

16. Build on the thoughts of those participating in the conversation. Your dialogue should paint a picture, so make sure all parties have a paintbrush.

APPENDIX 3

CHARACTERISTICS OF A PERSON OF EXCELLENCE

Appendix 3
Characteristics of A Person of Excellence

A Person of Excellence:

1. Delights in the prerequisite that brings him promotion.

2. Requires God's Word to evaluate his progress.

3. Keeps his word and never compromises his principles.
   "...[God] *honors those who fear the Lord; he who swears to his own hurt and does not change*" (Ps. 15:4).

4. Lives not in the hurts of yesterday, nor in the hopes of tomorrow, but in his present performance of excellence today.

5. Presses and stretches for the high road in every situation of life.
   "*I press toward the mark for the prize of the high calling of God in Christ Jesus*" (Phil. 3:14 *KJV*).

6. Is completely energized by the needs of others.
   "*Let each of you look out not only for his own interests, but also for the interests of others*" (Phil. 2:4).

7. Welcomes instruction.
   "*Give instruction to a wise man, and he will be still wiser; teach a just man, and he will increase in learning*" (Prov. 9:9).

8. Is not intimidated by correction.
   "Do not correct a scoffer, lest he hate you; rebuke a wise man, and he will love you" (Prov. 9:8).

9. Does not take correction personally.
   "Great peace have they which love thy law: and nothing shall offend them" (Ps. 119:165 *KJV*).

10. Refuses to adopt a "just good enough" attitude; instead, he presses on toward excellence when others say, "That's far enough."

11. Realizes that although others are the beneficiary of his excellence, Heaven is his only audience.
    "And whatever you do, do it heartily, as to the Lord and not to men" (Col. 3:23).

12. Discerns the gifts and talents of those around him so they can solve the problems God has assigned to them.

13. Doesn't try to impress everyone, but diligently works to impress a few.

14. Cannot be controlled or manipulated because he takes his direction from a higher authority.

15. Speaks to each person as if he were a king.
    "He who loves purity of heart and has grace on his lips, the king will be his friend" (Prov. 22:11).

16. Is kind and forgiving toward others because he knows that he himself has been forgiven.
    "And be ye kind one to another, tenderhearted, forgiving one another, even as God for Christ's sake hath forgiven you" (Eph. 4:32 *KJV*).

17. Treats others the way he wants to be treated — not the way others have treated him.

"And just as you want men to do to you, you also do to them likewise" (Luke 6:31).

18. Continually looks for the crossroads of change that will prepare him for his future.

19. Understands that his willingness to change demonstrates that he cares enough for others to become what they need him to be.

20. Doesn't get upset with what he is not in another person's life; instead, he maximizes who he is in that relationship.

21. Refuses to be disqualified by another person's flesh because he has fixed his eyes on God's promotion.

22. Believes that the smallest desire of those he serves is his greatest command.

23. Consistently reviews his instructions in order to evaluate his own performance.

24. Refuses shortcuts because he lives to do things the right way.

25. Is thankful for what others mean to him and continually expresses his gratitude.
    "I have not stopped giving thanks for you, remembering you in my prayers" (Eph. 1:16 *NIV*).

26. Continually upgrades his character.
    "But we all, with unveiled face, beholding as in a mirror the glory of the Lord, are being transformed into the same image from glory to glory, just as by the Spirit of the Lord" (2 Cor. 3:18).

27. Is good to all he comes in contact with but continually excels in his performance with the few to whom God has assigned him.

28. Is always standing at attention, waiting for his next instruction.

29. Is constantly adjusting himself to become what is needed without wearing his feelings on his sleeves.

30. Realizes the border of his own limitations.

31. Networks with others who are also pursuing excellence in order to inspire and to be inspired to become a better person.

32. Recognizes the gifts that others possess and then allows them room to grow and to express those gifts.

33. Evaluates what other people are not; then from the heart he becomes what is necessary.

34. Refuses to break focus because he realizes that others will pay the consequences.

A PERSON OF EXCELLENCE KNOWS:

35. That he can change his life by changing his attitudes. *"Your attitude should be the same as that of Christ Jesus"* (Phil. 2:5 *NIV*).

36. That it is never what is done to him that determines the outcome of his life; it is how he *responds* to what is done to him.

37. That he will only possess what he is willing to pursue.

38. That today's excellence is tomorrow's mediocrity; therefore, he doesn't let a day go by without change.

39. That every day he has to go from *conversation* to *demonstration* in his life.
"But he who looks into the perfect law of liberty and continues in it, and is not a forgetful hearer but a doer of the work, this one will be blessed in what he does" (James 1:25).

40. That sacrifice is the road he must travel on his journey to his destiny.
"...Any of you who does not give up everything he has cannot be my disciple" (Luke 14:33 *NIV*).

41. That the most important thing for him to learn is who he is as a believer.
"For you are all sons of God through faith in Christ Jesus" (Gal. 3:26).

42. That he has never "arrived"; therefore, he must keep sharpening his God-given gifts and talents.
"Not that I have already attained, or am already perfected; but I press on, that I may lay hold of that for which Christ Jesus has also laid hold of me" (Phil. 3:12).

43. That the people he closely associates with are the people he will be like.
"Do not be misled: 'Bad company corrupts good character'" (1 Cor. 15:33 *NIV*).

44. That someone greater than himself is always observing his every move to reward him.

45. That respect guarantees access.

46. That in all areas of life, he cannot correct what he is unwilling to confront.

47. That criticism is restricted to the power he gives it. *"In the shelter of your presence you hide them from the intrigues of men; in your dwelling you keep them safe from accusing tongues"* (Ps. 31:20 *NIV*).

48. That he cannot help people who think they know more than he does. *"...Knowledge puffs up, but love edifies"* (1 Cor. 8:1).

49. That when serving others, his own personal desires should never be anywhere to be seen.

50. That in order to enjoy relationships with others, he must be more interested in what others want than what *he* wants.

51. That his rewards come from the eternal; therefore, he has stopped looking for the temporal reward. *"...We look not at the things which are seen, but at the things which are not seen: for the things which are seen are temporal; but the things which are not seen are eternal"* (2 Cor. 4:18 *KJV*).

52. That not only does he have to pass his test with God; he has to qualify for greater responsibility and greater intimacy with his superiors before he is promoted.

53. That promotions come from God, but the timing of promotions is in the hands of men.

PRAYER OF SALVATION

Perhaps you have never been born again and therefore haven't even begun the pursuit of excellence in God. If you have never received Jesus Christ as your personal Lord and Savior and would like to do that right now, just pray this simple prayer:

Dear Lord Jesus, I know that I am lost and need Your forgiveness. I believe that You died for me on the Cross and that God raised You from the dead. I now invite You to come into my heart to be my Lord and Savior. Forgive me of all sin in my life and make me who You want me to be. Amen.

If you prayed this prayer from your heart, congratulations! You have just changed your destiny and will spend eternity with God. Your sins were forgiven the moment you made Jesus the Lord of your life. Now God sees you as pure and holy, as if you had never sinned. You have been set free from the bondage of sin!

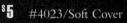
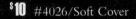

OTHER BOOKS BY ROBB THOMPSON

Victory Over Fear

The Winning Decision

You Are Healed

Marriage From God's Perspective

*The Great Exchange:
Your Thoughts for God's Thoughts*

Winning the Heart of God

Shattered Dreams

Excellence in Ministry

For a complete listing
of additional products
by Robb Thompson, please call:

**1-877-WIN-LIFE
(1-877-946-5433)**

You can also visit us on the web at:
www.winninginlife.org

To contact Robb Thompson, please write:

Robb Thompson
P. O. Box 558009
Chicago, Illinois 60655

Please include your prayer requests
and comments when you write.